HOMETOWN HUNTERS
COLLECTION

The Lost
Deer Camp

Lane Walker

Other books
in the Hometown Hunters Collection

The Legend of the Ghost Buck
The Hunt for Scarface
Terror on Deadwood Lake
The Boss on Redemption Road
The Day It Rained Ducks

The Lost Deer Camp
by Lane Walker
Copyright ©2016 Lane Walker

ISBN 978-0-9853548-5-5
For Worldwide Distribution
Printed in the U.S.A.

The Hometown Hunters Collection

www.lanewalkerbooks.com

Introduction

This book was written for the fans! Without you, Hometown Hunters wouldn't be possible. Thank you to every fan that has written or emailed me!

Knowing that kids across the country love my Hometown Hunters Collection makes all the late nights and hard work worth it.

Remember hard work makes the dream work! Just because you fall down, don't stay down! Who can? You can!

For His glory…

~ 1 ~

No....no, not now! I moaned as my flashlight died. I pounded the plastic bottom, hoping to get just a little more out of the cheap batteries I had bought at the gas station. I twisted and shook it until a faint yellow beam reappeared, casting an eerie yellow glow over the landscape.

This was the last place on earth I wanted to be without a light. I looked up at the full autumn moon poking through the trees and gazed at the brilliance of the stars through the cool crisp air. My breath was heavy and my heart still pounding from the encounter with the buck.

I thought the shot from my uncle's crossbow was good—I knew I had hit the buck. I found blood and was hot on the trail but I was tracking in uncharted waters, entering a place where I was forbidden to go.

Stupid light, I thought. It seemed like whenever I needed something the most, it would fail me.

I was deep in the dark, pine forest in the majestic Upper Peninsula of Michigan (or as the folks around here call it, the U.P.), a far cry from my home in Detroit.

I stumbled over a tree limb, just catching myself before falling headlong in the damp mud. Thankfully the moonlight that managed to make it through the tree branches cast enough light on the forest floor for me to make out the buck's tracks.

I was turned around, lost in a foreign land. I had no idea where I was or where I was going. That had been one of my major issues over the past four months. Not only was I lost, but I had a bigger problem. Uncle Ed had warned me to never enter the West Woods. He told me that it was off limits. In fact, whenever he talked about that part of the woods, his gentle voice changed, and there was fire in his eyes.

I assumed that it was because it was a bedding zone for the deer, a safe place. He was adamant,

"You can hunt anywhere you want, but stay out of the West Woods—*never* go near it."

I was happy that he let me hunt his 300 acres of paradise in the U.P filled with hardwoods, pines, and ridges, so I didn't argue. I was done arguing with people. But I was now officially farther into the West Woods than I had ever been.

Thanks to the full moon, I could make out faint shapes and shadows in the dark. I tried to look ahead to make sure I wasn't walking into a swamp or quicksand. There were strange stories about farmers losing cattle in the U.P. to some mysterious hidden quicksand. I wasn't sure if it was true, but I didn't want to find out. Ahead of me I noticed something strange, something that didn't fit with the tall white pines of the woods. It was swaying and moaning as though it were calling to me.

The strange motion of the object caught my eye and I was fixated on it. Even though I was scared, the curious side of me pushed me closer and closer. I wasn't following a blood trail anymore; the buck was the last thing on my mind.

As I got closer to the object, I could tell it was some type of wooden sign swaying in the October wind. The wind made it hard to make out the writing, but there was something written on it, some type of warning. My skin went cold and the hair on the back of my neck spiked as I ventured closer.

It was made of old barnwood and showed signs of wear. It had probably watched the forest grow around it. The forest canopy still blocked much of the moon, making it hard to read. I had to read it; I needed to know what it said. I pulled up my flashlight, praying that the batteries had just a little bit of life left in them.

I shook it and banged it hard against a nearby tree. When the flashlight flickered on, it was short-lived, but it gave me just enough time to read the sign's big, bold, blood red words: **Danger: Do Not Enter!**

~ 2 ~

Four months earlier I didn't know what hunting was and had never seen a wild, whitetail deer. There were only two things I knew—the concrete jungles of Detroit and baseball.

I had grown up and attended Easton Elementary on the north side of Detroit since kindergarten. It was a great school and I had lots of friends. Life was simple and easy.

I was an honor roll student and loved baseball. Pitching was my favorite thing and I was good at it. Our family traveled all around Michigan during the spring, while I played in various baseball tournaments. I had a strong arm and a nasty curve ball. My nickname was Tucker the Terrible because other kids hated trying to bat against me.

When I didn't pitch, I played second base. My dad was always my coach, Mom kept the stats, and my sister, Tina, was our official cheerleader. Although she is a couple years younger than I am she too enjoyed the days spent on the dusty diamonds. Life seemed great, until one summer day changed everything.

It was the last day of school of my seventh grade year. Tina and I were excited and more than ready for summer vacation. I cleaned out my locker for the last time, preparing to leave Easton Elementary for good. Next year I would be attending Hilltop Middle School. It was the same school my parents had attended and where most of my friends were going. While I was sad to leave Easton, I was ready to see what adventures I could have at Hilltop.

Tina and I practically ran home. School was officially over—no more homework, just sunshine, swimming, and baseball.

Something wasn't right as we turned onto our block and saw our house. Both of our parents cars were in the driveway, which was unusual.

"I wonder why they didn't pick us up from school," I said, turning to Tina.

Mom worked at the local bank, and Dad worked as a diesel mechanic, fixing big semi-trucks. He never got home before 5:00, so I was surprised to see both of them sitting at the kitchen table when we walked in.

I will never forget the look on their faces. All the excitement of the last day of school dumped out of my body. My stomach started to turn and hurt—something was terribly wrong.

"Tucker, Tina, have a seat. We need to talk," Dad said. His voice was cold and distant.

Mom's head was down. It was obvious she had been crying.

Dad inhaled and drew a deep breath and exhaled slowly.

"There's no easy way to do this, so I'm just going to say it. Your mom and I are getting divorced," he finally said.

~ 3 ~

A divorce? That was something I definitely wasn't expecting. They argued once in a while, but I never thought it was anything major.

His words burned through my soul! Tina started crying, but I would expect that out of a fourth grader. I wasn't going to well up, since eighth grade guys don't cry. They tried explaining the why and how, but I didn't listen. They mentioned that the divorce wouldn't be final until sometime around Christmas, but it didn't matter to me. As far as I was concerned, it was already over. Our family was done, everything I knew and loved was gone.

I ran up to my room without saying a word. I had a lot of questions but was filled with so much anger I just wanted to be left alone. I threw myself down on my bed, fighting back the tears, asking myself how they could do this to our family. My feelings flipped between anger and sadness. How could they do this to me? Tina?

After an hour there was a soft knock on my door.

"Tucker, can we talk?" asked Dad.

My dad wasn't too much of an emotional guy, and talking wasn't one of his strong points. In fact, besides his love for baseball, he was usually a reserved, quiet guy.

I didn't know what to say. I just sat staring at the ceiling. It was an awkward silence, like nothing I'd ever experienced before. I wasn't going to say anything, I decided, he was the one that did this. I wanted to make it as hard on him as I could.

He talked for about five minutes. He made up a bunch of excuses and tried to explain why it would be better this way. He told me how they didn't get along and that they both agreed it would be better to be separated. I wasn't buying it and he knew it.

When he was done, he got up to leave. That

was the last time he would talk about the divorce to me. He must have thought he had covered everything and I understood. In his mind, he felt like he had done his job and now everything would be just fine. Well, it wasn't.

Just before shutting my door, he stopped. There was one more thing he had on his mind.

"Tucker, get yourself together, we have baseball practice in an hour," said Dad.

Baseball? Does he think I care about baseball right now? Those words shot right through me. I couldn't believe he thought that much about a stupid game.

I decided to quit playing baseball. Right then I made up my mind I wouldn't throw another pitch that summer. *That will teach him to give up on his family,* I thought.

Dad couldn't believe it when he came back into my room and I was still laying there.

"I said, let's go, Tucker. The team is waiting for you."

I just turned my back and buried my head in my pillow. Dad was known all around the Detroit area as one of the greatest baseball coaches. Now his prize pitcher was throwing in the towel and calling it quits. I knew that would cut him deeper than anything I could say.

He mumbled something as he slammed the door. I had gotten his attention without even saying a word. Not only did I not plan on playing baseball, I also had no plans on talking to my dad.

The months that followed were the worst months of my entire life. From that day forward, my entire life changed.

The next week Dad moved out to a small townhouse a couple miles away. I couldn't believe how empty our house felt. It seemed like the house was a shell, and we were just taking up space; it was no longer a home.

Mom had to work even harder and struggled balancing being a single mom with her job. I mostly just hung out in my room and listened to music. I stayed up half the night and slept almost all day. The warm weather I loved so much became a distant memory. I stopped wearing sports related clothing and started wearing basic black. Part of it was because I was too lazy to wash my own clothes and the other reason was that I was protesting. I was going to let the world know how dark my life was.

Deep down, inside my soul, I missed baseball, but I would never let on to Dad or anyone else. Tina and I went to his townhouse every other weekend. It was boring and I hated it. It felt so strange to not see my parents together.

In the past, I never wanted summer to end; I wanted baseball season to last forever, but not this summer. September couldn't come soon enough. I had nothing to look forward to—it was the summer without a season. This was the first summer I was counting down the days, excited to go back to school. Since I hadn't played baseball, I didn't see a lot of my friends. Most of my teammates were my closest friends, and I had pulled myself away from them.

It was probably better because I wasn't myself. I wasn't the same person; I had changed. I turned into a loner. The team guy in me was all but gone.

In late August, with two weeks of summer vacation left, Mom dropped another bombshell on us. Just when I thought things couldn't get worse, she proved me wrong.

"We're moving," she said.

Moving? What? Now? Like dealing with the divorce wasn't horrible enough, now were going to leave the only place I had ever known. I always blamed my dad for the divorce, now I was angry with my mom for making us move.

Going to Hilltop Middle School was the only thing I looked forward to, the only thing I cared about.

She went on to explain how she couldn't afford the house with having only one income. She also struggled keeping our three-bedroom house clean and felt like this was the best idea for everyone. She said we all needed a fresh start, but all I heard were more adult excuses.

No matter what she said, I knew what she really meant. "I don't care what you think or how you feel—I'm the one in charge."

- 4 -

We were moving into a two-bedroom apartment on the other side of Detroit, the east side. It
was worlds away from where we lived now. She
might as well have moved us to another planet.

I would be attending Washington Carver
Middle School—an inner city school known for
having tough kids and lots of issues.

Over the next two weeks, they packed and I
hid in my room. Every day the house got emptier
and emptier, just like I felt. On moving day there
were no pictures left hanging on the wall. I
looked over at the corner of the living room and
remembered the place where we always put up
our Christmas tree. I wandered into the kitchen
and opened the pantry. An empty weight hit me
hard. I looked at all the ink pen marks on the
pantry door where we charted our growth. That

wasn't our door anymore; this wasn't my home. Someone new would own the door and all its memories.

I slipped my headphones on, threw on my backpack, and walked out the front door without looking back. I was leaving the last piece of my heart in that old house.

It took us about thirty minutes to drive to our new place. It wasn't that far away, but we had to drive through Detroit traffic.

We pulled into Whispering Winds Apartment complex on the corner of Martin Luther King Boulevard and Seeger Street. The apartment complex reminded me of a giant beehive. There were people of every color and cars everywhere, no lawn, no baseball diamond, just concrete. Cement and asphalt went as far as the eye could see.

It started to get dark as we unloaded the car. Our new home was now Apartment K-3. We didn't even have our own address anymore; we shared one with 200 tenants. How sad, to be labeled by one letter and number.

Dad didn't even help us move, I thought, *at*

least he would help us unload some of the heavy stuff. How could he make us do it alone? It didn't matter now, I was going to have to be the man of the house. The blackness inside my heart was spreading, and I was becoming harder and harder by the day.

By the time we were done unpacking, I was exhausted. I carried the last box up the three flights of stairs and sat it down on the kitchen table.

"Well I guess that's a day. You better get some sleep; school starts tomorrow," said Mom.

The next morning I was going to start another adventure. Mom did everything she could to make Washington Carver Middle School sound great. But I knew better; that school would never be great. Nothing was going to help or make me feel better. That night I made up my mind, I was going to leave a lasting impression on W.C. Middle School. They were going to know right away who Tucker Thompson was.

It was time for the return of Tucker the Terrible, but only this time the nickname had nothing to do with baseball.

I was still worn out from all the moving and had trouble getting up the next morning. I didn't have the usual excitement most kids have about the first day of school.

The day was starting off a lot like my life, horrible, and it wasn't going to get any better. I was going to make sure of that.

~ 5 ~

My sister was excited and had picked out her outfit the night before. Tina didn't seem too affected by the divorce; she was still a happy kid as long as she had cartoons and fruit punch juice boxes.

Our first day of school, and we were already running behind, but that was something I was going to get used to. Tina was so mad at Mom because being late was the last thing she wanted on her first day at a new school.

In all honesty, I was the reason we were late, but I found it funny that she blamed Mom. I blamed Mom for a lot of things, so it didn't bother me. Tina was going to attend an elementary school a couple blocks away from Washington Carver.

Mom wanted to walk Tina to class so she

dropped me off first. As we pulled up, the differences between Hilltop and Washington Carver were obvious. There were lots of kids, way more than I had ever seen. There were kids from every ethnic background, but most kids were African American.

Giant stone steps greeted students and I could tell the school was old. Mom wished me good luck as I slammed the door. She didn't deserve a goodbye, and I knew luck had nothing to do with it. It was her fault I was there.

Looking around I noticed a big man standing near the front door at the top of the steps. I wasn't sure who he was, but I could tell he was someone in authority. He was huge, muscular, and had a serious look on his face. He wore a black suit and a fancy tie. He had to be at least 6 foot 6 inches and weighed well over 300 pounds. I knew he was just the man I was looking for.

Even though Washington Carver was full of excitement, it seemed like everyone was staring at me as I walked up the steps. I was the new kid. I knew this was my chance to make a good first impression.

"Welcome to Washington Carver Middle School, home of the Titans," said the man as I walked towards the front door.

I smiled and nodded sticking my hand out to shake his. Just as he reached for mine, I pulled it away and walked into the school.

"Too slow, Big Guy," I said as I sauntered through the front door. I could tell he wasn't impressed, so I got the response that I wanted. I took two more steps before hearing his loud, bellowing voice.

"My office, now!" His voice shook the hallways and everyone stopped in their tracks. But I knew he was talking to me. That's exactly what I wanted.

I walked down the hall and saw a sign pointing to the office. I went in and sat down.

"Can I help you?" the secretary asked.

"The big guy out front sent me in here," I said with a smile.

The secretary's face squinted, "That big guy out front is our principal, Mr. David. You must be new to Washington Carver."

Good, he was just the man I was looking for.

About five minutes later, Mr. David walked in. He had a certain presence about him; there was no doubt he was in charge. He was an African American, someone that obviously took great pride in his role at W.C. Middle School.

"My office," he thundered and pointed to a wooden door behind the front desk.

I got up and walked in as he followed me through the door. He slammed the door behind us.

"Tucker, I want to be very clear about how we do things at Washington Carver," said Mr. David. I had no doubt that he was a former military man, maybe a Marine or Navy Seal.

He would have easily given any normal eighth grader nightmares but not me. The new me wasn't going to be scared of anyone or anything. I had already been through the worst three months of my life; there was nothing he was going to do worse than that.

His office was full of all kinds of football memorabilia—a bunch of pictures of former students from Washington Carver who went on to play football in college and tons of Green Bay Packer stuff.

Being a Detroit kid, I hated the Packers. It made me hate Mr. David even more. It was weird hating someone that I didn't know, but I was getting good at it.

I was surprised he already knew my name. There had to be 1,000 kids at Washington Carver.

"Whatever," I muttered back.

"Whatever?," he demanded.

"You got rules; I get it," I said.

"No, I don't think you do. At Washington Carver, it's my way or the highway!" he said pounding his fist on his desk.

"The highway sounds pretty good to me," I said.

He didn't like that. I could tell he wasn't used to someone being so mouthy, especially someone new to the school.

He took a long, deep breath and leaned back in his chair. I could tell he was trying to calm himself down.

"This is your first day, so consider this a warning. No one talks that way to me or anyone else here. You are a Titan now; act like it. Have a good day, Tucker," he said.

"Sure," I said with a smile. Walking out, I wondered what he meant when he said I was a Titan. Who said I wanted to be part of his stupid school? A Titan? I didn't even know what a Titan was.

I wanted to make a lasting impression, one that Mr. David wouldn't forget. I had no plans on following his rules or listening to anyone.

As I walked out I noticed a sign hanging above the door, **TITAN:** *A person or thing of very great strength, intellect, or importance.*

I wasn't going to be a Titan; I definitely didn't fit that bill.

- 6 -

My first day at Washington Carver was both horrible and perfect at the same time. I was late for almost every one of my classes, I was pretty sure all the teachers already hated me. I had no idea where I was going, and I forgot my locker combination twice.

I knew none of this would have happened at Hilltop; none of this would have happened if Mom and Dad hadn't gotten divorced.

Every day I attended Washington Carver Middle School, it fueled my anger towards my parents as well as myself. During the first month of school, I was written up twelve times. Most of the time, it was for being disrespectful or sleeping in class.

That whole time I hadn't made any friends, except Bryce Kipper. We weren't really even friends, more like competitors. We were both troublemakers and were in a constant competition to see who could have the most disciplinary write-ups. It was the only thing I enjoyed about school. I had twelve; he had eleven.

Mr. David watched me like a hawk. One thing I did love about W.C. Middle School was they had to call home every time a student was sent to the office. I loved it. I wanted them to have to stop their day and hear how bad I was.

We had several meetings at school with Mr. David and the counselor. My parents told them how I was having a hard time because of the divorce, how I had so much potential, blah, blah, blah.

They liked to remind me of how good I used to be. But every time they said it, it just made me more angry. Anytime they sat me down to talk, I just sat there without responding. Not talking was the one thing they couldn't take away or make me change. I don't think it even crossed their minds that they were the reason I kept getting in trouble.

I wanted to tell them about how empty I was,

about how much I hurt. But I didn't. I wanted to go back to Hilltop, I wanted everything back to normal. I wanted my mom and dad to make everything right again. I wanted them to get back together. I wasn't going to stop until that happened.

My little shenanigans weren't working; they were too basic. I knew I had to do something drastic to really get their attention, to make them see what both of them had done to me. But what could I do?

I needed a show stopper, one that would put me on the map forever at W.C., something that would even shock the unshakable Mr. David.

The idea finally came to me when I was sitting in Mr. Field's history class. We were watching some documentary about World War II. I wasn't paying attention, instead I was looking out the window towards the football field. There was a P.E. class playing a flag football game on the main lawn.

It was late October and Friday was homecoming. The whole school was buzzing with excitement about the annual homecoming game versus our crosstown rival, East Tech Middle School.

I leaned over and whispered to Bryce, "You ready to make history?"

At first he was reluctant to join my plan. I had a plan; I think Bryce was just jealous because he hadn't thought of it.

Mr. David had no idea what was coming to Washington Carver. No one did.

~ 7 ~

Time was moving slowly as I counted down the days to Friday. Our eighth grade football team was always undefeated and had a rich, historic tradition. They were a powerhouse, a football force to be reckoned with and known throughout Detroit. In fact, one day I heard Mr. David lecturing a new student about the prowess of his football team. He mentioned they hadn't lost a game in over three years. I had heard from Bryce that Mr. David was some former hero at Washington Carver years ago when he attended the school.

I hated the football players. They were cocky and acted like they owned the school. I think the main reason I didn't like them was because I knew I was better than most of them.

Even though baseball was my sport, I was a better quarterback than the one they had. I was even picked over the starting quarterback during P.E. class.

I had a great arm from all the years of baseball. Some of the guys encouraged me to play at first, but once they saw how I acted, those requests stopped coming. There was a part of me that really wanted to play; I loved competition. But I couldn't, I wasn't going to give my dad the satisfaction. He would think everything was okay and that he had a right to act like a dad again. I pictured him on the bleachers smiling as his son did something good. He would think I was happy.

The hallway was decorated for homecoming, and there were signs up everywhere. Kids were talking about the homecoming assembly that was planned for Friday afternoon. It was a big deal at W.C. The students and staff played all kinds of fun games that they had been doing for over fifty years. Everyone dressed in their red and black Titan gear.

On Wednesday, Bryce came to me during lunch and I could tell something was wrong.

"Tucker, I don't know, man," he said.

"You don't know about what?" I demanded.

He looked around and leaned in.

"About Friday," he whispered.

Bryce was getting cold feet and that was the last thing I needed. My plan wouldn't work without his help. I had to think quickly.

"No problem, Bryce. I already talked to Jimmy Nix and he wants to do it. You can chicken out," I said, lying through my teeth.

I hadn't talked to Jimmy because I already knew he wouldn't do it.

I quickly added, "It would probably be better anyway. That way I will have two more write-ups than you; I will be in the record books after Friday. No one will ever remember you, but I know they won't forget me," I said.

That was all it took. Bryce took a huge bite of his peanut butter and banana sandwich.

"Fine. I'll be ready," he blurted out.

The next couple of days I laid low and tried to keep out of Mr. David's crosshairs.

I had asked Mom to make her famous meatloaf on Thursday night. It's one of my favorite meals so

Mom didn't think anything was out of the ordinary. That night I went to bed and set my alarm to go off fifteen minutes earlier than normal.

I couldn't afford to sleep in or be late on Friday. I jumped up startled when my alarm went off. It read 6:05 and it took me a minute to remember why I was getting up so early.

I wiped the crud out of my eyes and got dressed. I tiptoed to the fridge and pulled out the leftover meatloaf from the night before. I reached in and pulled out ketchup, mayonnaise, and some pickles. I dumped everything into the blender and cut a huge piece of meatloaf.

I held the lid down and hit the button. The sound made me lurch as I held down the lid for ten seconds, just enough time to blend and mash everything together.

"Tucker is that you?" groaned mom from her bedroom.

"Yeah, it is. Sorry about the noise. I'm making a breakfast shake," I said.

"Since when do you get up early enough to eat breakfast?"

She was right. I very seldom ate breakfast.

"Starting today, I'm trying to eat heathy," I replied, hoping to stop her questions.

I waited for a minute and realized she had bought my story. I took out two glass Mason jars from the cupboard and put the concoction into the jars.

I went back to my bedroom and wrapped the jars in an old t-shirt. I didn't want them to break in my backpack.

I had big plans for Mom's meatloaf and for the Titan's homecoming.

~ 8 ~

"Good morning, Mr. David," I said, smiling as I entered W.C. Middle School. He was decked in red, black, and white Titan gear from head to toe.

He half smiled and looked at me quizzically. We didn't have the best relationship. I don't think he liked my sense of humor. I had given him nothing but grief since I arrived at W.C. I walked towards my locker and waited for Bryce. The bell rang and the hall started to empty as most of the students made their way to their first hour class.

Two minutes later, the hall was completely empty and still no sign of Bryce.

I put my backpack in my locker and started to walk towards my first hour math class. I knew Mrs. Ziel would have a fun math test ready to help celebrate homecoming. I was walking fast, the last thing I needed was another tardy. I didn't want Mrs. Ziel to send me to Mr. David's office because I needed to steer clear of him right now. I would be visiting him soon enough.

I walked into class and sat down just as the tardy bell rang. Mrs. Ziel looked at me and seemed disappointed that I was there. I think she was hoping I was absent so she could enjoy her day and the school homecoming.

It was hard to concentrate on her Fun Friday test. I couldn't believe that Bryce was backing out.

What a wimp....

The bell finally rang and I went to my locker to get my history book for second hour. I carefully reached in my backpack searching for my book. I could feel the cold jars rattling around.

I felt a firm hand on my shoulder. I closed my eyes, assuming it was Mr. David.

Did Bryce rat me out?

I slowly pulled my hand out of my backpack trying to keep the jars from clanking together.

I turned and to my relief it was Bryce.

"Sorry, Tucker, I missed the bus," he said. He

was dressed in some grungy old jeans and a grey shirt. I think Bryce and I were the only ones in the entire school that didn't have something Titan on. This seemed fitting because we were the only ones who weren't Titans.

"You ready?" I whispered.

He nodded and I reached in and grabbed one of the jars, handing it to him. He tucked the jar in his shirt and walked over to his locker.

We made eye contact and then went our separate ways. He was ready; I could tell he was actually going to go through with it. I sat through my next two classes in a daze, waiting for lunch. It couldn't come soon enough.

When the bell rang dismissing third hour, I pulled out the brown paper bag that was holding my jar and started towards the lunchroom.

The cafeteria was noisy and full of happiness. All the football players were wearing their white and red jerseys, strutting around like some movie stars.

I walked towards the back of the cafeteria near the stage and sat down.

Bryce walked in and positioned himself at the front of the cafeteria.

Everything was set. It was time to start our homecoming festivities.

~ 9 ~

I waited until 11:50. It had to be that exact time because that was when all the eighth graders were in the lunchroom. Besides Bryce, no one ever sat with me so it didn't look strange for me to be by myself.

I reached my hand down into the brown tattered lunch bag and slowly pulled out the jar. I bent down and turned so my back was to the students as I screwed off the lid.

The smell was terrible. I had to stop myself from actually puking.

I inhaled taking one deep breath and turned. BLAHHHHHHHH! I made the most disgusting gagging sound I could while throwing the contents of the jar in the air. In slow motion I watched as the mixture of meatloaf, ketchup, mayo, and other ingredients from my fridge flew through the air. It looked just like real puke. As soon as my evil concoction hit the ground, Bryce opened his, made a disgusting puking sound, and threw his jar all over the floor.

What happened next is hard to describe in words. But staff and students at Washington Carver Middle School will remember the image forever.

It started slowly with only a couple kids at first. Subtle, quiet gagging noises were spreading throughout the cafeteria. Then in an instant, one student lost it and actually threw up all over his table.

That was all it took; the chain effect took over. Within seconds, kids started throwing up all over the cafeteria, and total chaos ensued.

Kids were running for the bathrooms, slipping on puke; even the kitchen workers took off running, trying to escape the mess.

I watched as Jesse Hancock, the football team's star running back puked all over his pristine, white Titan jersey.

Rumor had it that by the time the dust cleared;

almost every football player had stained their Titan uniform.

I wouldn't know; I didn't wait around to see how it unfolded. I walked out of the cafeteria right to the main office.

"Why are you here, Tucker?" Mrs. Forester asked.

I smiled, "I have a feeling Mr. David will want to see me," I said.

Five minutes later the office door flew open! In walked Mr. David, his white Titan polo covered in smelly puke. His shoes squeaked from all the throw up on the cafeteria floor. He didn't even make eye contact with me as he marched to his office. He slammed the door so hard I thought the hinges were going to rip away from the door frame.

I knew I had needed to do something epic, something that would get everyone's attention forever. I sat and waited. I knew the next two people that would be walking through the door would be my parents. I just hoped I had done enough to get both of their attention.

This was something neither of them could hide from, maybe this time they would stop being mad at each other.

- 10 -

Twenty minutes later, I saw my mom's black four door Ford pull up to the front entrance of the school. Two minutes later, my dad's truck screeched to a halt.

A part of me smiled because this was one of the first times since the divorce when they were actually together.

I sat up a little straighter when they both walked in but not much. I was prepared for a serious tongue lashing but didn't get one. They both looked at me and without saying a word walked directly to Mr. David's office.

Yikes! I didn't expect that; for a split second I wondered if I had gone a little too far with my prank. I reassured myself it was just what needed to happen to get them both here, both to talk again.

Plus, I couldn't help but laugh at all the football players. The thought of them running out on the field in their white, puke stained Titan uniforms made me chuckle.

I thought it would be over quickly. In fact, I had rehearsed my lines. I was going to apologize and tell them both how much the divorce affected me. I was finally ready to talk, ready to tell them how I felt.

Before I knew it, they had been in Mr. David's office for over thirty minutes. I wondered what they were talking about.

What was the worst that could happen? I could get a ten-day suspension or have to find another school. All of those options didn't seem bad to me.

The door finally opened and Mr. David motioned for me to enter his office. I had to bite my lip to not laugh out loud; he still had some puke on the corner of his shirt.

I didn't think smiling would help my case with my parents, so I put on a wooden face, walked in, and sat down. There was an obvious look of disappointment on Mom and Dad's faces. I tried not to make eye contact with them.

"Tucker, we are all deeply disappointed with your little stunt today. You have ruined our Titan homecoming by doing the unthinkable!" Mr. David said.

He was fuming mad; I had never seen him so frustrated. There was a large vein throbbing on his forehead when he spoke.

Before I could say a word, he added, "We have been nothing but nice to you. I know you have a lot of stuff going on in your life, but your behavior at Washington Carver Middle School is inexcusable!"

Now was my chance because I had an excuse, a good one too. I was going to tell him and my parents how the divorce had ruined my life and how much I hated each of them for breaking up our family. I had waited all summer to do it. It was finally my turn to talk; this was my chance.

"Well actually—" I began quietly.

"Be quiet, Tucker, he's not done!" snarled my dad.

"But—" I tried to say.

"Not a word!" my mother snapped, glaring at me.

I slouched back down in my chair. That was the first time in my life my mom had ever raised her voice to me.

"Tucker, you are no longer welcome at Washington Carver Middle School," Mr. David declared forcefully.

"Good!" I thought maybe now they would find a way to get me back to Hilltop.

"Tucker, your mom and I have made a tough decision. You're going to go live with your Great Uncle Ed and Aunt Loretta," Dad said in a quiet voice.

What? Who?

My plan quickly unraveled. The thought of them sending me away never even crossed my mind. I barely knew my Uncle Ed and Aunt Loretta. I saw them like once a year at Christmas or some other cheesy family event.

Then I remembered they lived in the Upper Peninsula. I had never been out of Detroit. They lived in a tiny town south of Escanaba called Plainsville—a town with about ten people and one blinking light.

I would rather they sent me to a jail or some kind of boot camp for bad kids. From Detroit to Plainsville—it sounded like a sick joke. I was headed to the backwoods of Michigan to live with two people I barely knew.

My stunt had worked. I was famous, I had gotten Mr. David's attention and brought my parents together. But instead of fixing anything, I just was sentenced to death—death in the U.P.

I got a one-way ticket to nowhere. Now I would be even further away from my parents and their problems.

~ 11 ~

"Go pack your stuff now!" Mom said as she slammed shut the front door of our apartment.

I rushed to my room and started throwing clothes in my suitcase. I was so mad. I hadn't even gotten to talk to both of my parents together.

I walked over to my dresser and started packing up some video games.

"You won't be needing those. Uncle Ed isn't big into technology so you might as well leave all that junk here," Mom said.

What am I going to do in the middle of nowhere without any electronics or games? Why did they have to torture me even more? I grabbed my suitcase and dragged it down the hallway, yelling things at my mom.

I stopped just before heading out and looked around. I wasn't sure if I would ever be back.

But it didn't matter, this tiny apartment wasn't my home. For the first time in my life, I didn't have one—I was homeless.

I hurried outside and opened the door to Mom's car.

"Tucker, not this time, your dad is going to take you," Mom yelled from the porch. I could tell she was starting to cry. My anger died down a little bit as she walked down the stairs and hugged me. She held my face and told me she loved me as I turned away. I walked over and threw my suitcase in the cab of Dad's truck and climbed in.

Then I saw my parents talk together for the first time since that day they told us they were getting divorced. It wasn't the type of conversation I had hoped for. I couldn't believe how cold the conversation looked. It was more like strictly business, like Dad was trying to sell a car to someone or close a business deal. It was emotionless; there was no love left between them.

The once high school sweethearts that had been married fifteen years were now just associates. They didn't even play on the same team anymore. They were just working together because they had no other choice. The only thing they had in common was Tina and I.

Dad crawled into the truck and slammed the door. I just looked straight ahead and within a couple minutes we were turning onto I-75 to start our trek north.

As we were driving down the highway, a thought hit me. Life can be so ironic. Here we were traveling down I-75 but heading north instead of south. Usually Michiganders take I-75 south to Florida for a vacation that meant a great family time. But we weren't going on a vacation.

"We got a long trip, Tucker, why don't you rest."

I still hadn't said a word to Dad. He was the person that made me the angriest.

I was worn out and tired. I closed my eyes and leaned my head against the window. The humming of the truck slowly rocked me to sleep.

I woke up a couple hours later just before Gaylord. There was a big bulletin board advertising Jay's Sporting Goods. The sign had a huge whitetail buck on it and listed all their fall hunting deals. I had never hunted, but it was something I always wanted to try. I closed my eyes again, hoping everything was just an awful nightmare.

I woke up to my dad poking me in the side.

"I didn't think you'd want to miss this," he said.

I cleared my eyes just in time to see a huge bridge in the distance. It was magnificent!

The blue beams rose above the water and it appeared to be reaching up to heaven. I had never seen anything so grand. The truck hummed across the bridge as I gazed out the window. The deep blue waters of Lake Michigan shone bright and brilliant.

I had never seen the Mackinac Bridge in person, only in my history book. The Mighty Mac didn't disappoint me, and I was in awe as we drove across the fifth largest suspension bridge in the world. The rest of the bridge loomed on the horizon, giving it an endless appearance.

The splendor of the Mackinac Bridge hypnotized me, taking away some of my anger but only for a little while.

~ 12 ~

Picasso or Michelangelo couldn't have painted a better picture than the view from the bridge.

The shoreline was littered with the most amazing splashes of color. I had never seen so many hues of red, orange, and yellow. The trees had such a magical glow, there was no doubt fall was in full swing. I remember one of my teachers in elementary school telling the class how she had spent the weekend on a color tour in the Upper Peninsula. She described the endless beauty and amazing colors, but even her description didn't do it justice. I had never seen anything so gorgeous. The fall trees marked our entrance to the U.P.

We didn't have views like that in Detroit. My moment of peace was interrupted by Dad.

"I just don't get you, Tucker. I think a lot of this has to do with you quitting baseball." Dad's voice brought me back to reality.

I still hadn't said a word to him since we left Detroit. I just kept staring out the window, never acknowledging he even spoke to me.

Baseball? He thinks this is about stupid baseball. I wanted to scream in his face, it is because of YOU! YOU did this, baseball has nothing to do with it. YOU gave up on your family! YOU didn't fight for mom, for any of us! YOU quit, not me!

I wasn't ready to talk to him, and it wasn't because I didn't know what to say. It was because I had too much to tell him. It was because I hated him. I already had a headache from the day's events, and I didn't want to get into another argument.

When I heard his voice, it was almost like the beautiful leaves died and turned an ugly black and were dead, rotten on the inside. I knew exactly how each one of those leaves felt.

Dad just stared ahead, his foot firmly on the pedal.

~ 13 ~

The sun slowly faded behind the horizon and the sky turned a smoky gray and then black. I wasn't sure how long we had been on the road. I had fallen asleep a couple times after crossing the bridge.

The red glow of the truck radio read 7:45, so I figured we had been on the road about six hours. It was around eleven when I pulled the puking prank and about 1:00 when we left our apartment.

I was tired and hungry, I was hoping Dad was going to stop along the way to get some food, but he wasn't in the mood to eat.

Even after the puke prank, I still had an appetite. Now I wish I would have at least eaten lunch at school before I was kicked out.

Dad was on a mission. I was sure he wanted to

get rid of me as soon as he could. We had already turned off the highway onto US-2 a couple hours back. A big orange and black sign lit up the night sky. "Welcome to Escanaba, Home of the Eskymos" greeted us as we pulled into town. Escanaba was bigger than most of the other towns we had passed through in the U.P.

Dad put on his blinker and headed west on Highway 2. The bright lights faded behind us as he drove back into the vastness of the Upper Peninsula.

I knew we had to be close to Uncle Ed's, but how close I didn't know and wasn't about to ask. We quietly passed through the tiny town of Bark River and kept traveling west.

Ten minutes later, Dad turned onto Cedar Ridge Road and we drove another twenty minutes north. At first we passed a couple houses lit with warm porch lights but as we went further, the lights faded, and there were only a handful of houses.

Dad's blinker caught me off guard as we finally turned onto a makeshift gravel driveway. I couldn't believe how isolated Uncle Ed and Aunt Loretta's house was. In Detroit, neighbors were everywhere, always an arm's length away.

As we drove towards the house, I could see a figure sitting on the front porch, rocking slowly in a chair. I laughed on the inside; it reminded me of everything I thought the country was like.

When Dad's truck came to an abrupt halt, I opened the door to the smell of a wood burning stove puffing its smoke up and out the old chimney. The odor was pungent and hung in the air.

I quickly noticed how modest the house was. It was smaller than most houses in Detroit, not much bigger than our apartment.

The last time I had seen Uncle Ed, he was a weathered old man, with a plump belly and glowing white hair. He would have looked just like Santa Claus if he had a beard. I was glad he didn't because I don't think I would have been able to stop myself from laughing at the sight. And now was definitely not the time to laugh.

"Howdy folks!" Uncle Ed said, welcoming us to his place.

I nodded and Dad thanked him for agreeing to let me stay. I just stared at the house, wondering how long I would have to live in the middle of nowhere.

"I think Tucker just needs a little time with his Great Uncle Ed," he said with a boyish smile. When I looked at him, there was something soothing about him. He seemed like a genuinely kind man. Just being in his presence was calming. I knew I couldn't be rude or disrespectful to him—he didn't have anything to do with the divorce.

It was strange, I had never been intimidated by big, hulking Mr. David. But there was something about Uncle Ed's mannerisms that made me instantly respect him.

"Who's hungry? I have homemade soup and fresh apple pie for desert," a sweet voice from the front door asked.

"Let's go break bread, son, it's not good to keep your Aunt Loretta waiting," said Uncle Ed.

- 14 -

Aunt Loretta's food was amazing! The fancy restaurants in Detroit couldn't hold a candle to her cooking. It was the best food I had ever tasted.

I couldn't remember the last time I sat down with people and ate a meal together. Everyone was too busy in Detroit.

Dad had left quickly after dropping me off since he had a long drive back home. I never said a word to him, not even goodbye.

Uncle Ed could tell I was hungry, and there was a little small talk during our late dinner but not much. Their house was cozy and warm. The woodstove provided a dry, warm heat. I liked the smell of the wood as it burnt in the fireplace. The temperature had dropped as we drove up north, and I was glad they had the warm fire.

"You better head off to bed," Uncle Ed said after we finished.

I looked down at my watch and saw it was only 10:30. I couldn't remember the last time I had gone to bed before midnight. Tonight I didn't mind though, I was exhausted from the day's events.

"Early morning tomorrow; we got to cut some wood. I will wake you up at 5:30 for breakfast," said Uncle Ed.

Breakfast at 5:30 on a Saturday morning? I hadn't gotten up that early on a weekend, not once that I could remember in my entire life!

There was nothing appealing about cutting wood, but I just nodded in agreement. I didn't want to start off on the wrong foot. Plus, I didn't figure I had many options. I was stuck in the middle of nowhere and couldn't have gone anywhere even if I wanted to. I was completely lost.

"Tucker, I have your bed made. The first room on the right is yours," Aunt Loretta said as she led me down the hall. If Uncle Ed was a saint, Aunt Loretta was an angel. Her voice was sweet and her eyes were full of life. I thanked her for a fine dinner and went into my new bedroom. I had no idea how long I'd be staying here, but I figured I would try to make the best of it while I was there.

The room had some old football posters and other sports stuff on the wall. The bedding was completely Green Bay Packers from the pillow cases to the sheets. When I looked around, I saw that everything was Packer related in the room.

Dad always told me that Yooper's are huge Packer Fans. (A Yooper is what we Detroiters call anyone that lives in the Upper Peninsula.)

I changed into some gym shorts and crawled into bed. The bed was a little lumpy but still comfortable. When my head hit the pillow, I let out a big yawn. I fell asleep so fast I didn't have time to feel sorry for myself.

"Tucker, Tucker, wake up," Uncle Ed said pulling at my arm. I was in a deep sleep and flinched when I saw the big, burly outline of my uncle standing over me. For a minute, I had forgotten where I was.

I sat up and wiped the drool from my mouth. What in the world was that smell? The wonderful aroma filled the air and grabbed my attention. Bacon! The sweet smell of bacon was streaming in from the kitchen. I got up and went to the kitchen. The table was set and there was a big platter full of homemade pancakes, sausage, and bacon.

I sat down and the strong aromas forced me to smile. I couldn't remember the last time I had such a great breakfast. I usually didn't eat breakfast, and if I did, I mostly ate potato chips. I couldn't believe how much I ate, especially after last night's feast.

After the meal Uncle Ed brought some insulated bibs and a heavy coat and put them by my chair.

"You might need these," he said. He only had a pair of pants and a light jacket on. But once I stepped outside, I was so glad to have on the extra clothes. It was freezing outside!

We started walking back into the giant hardwoods behind Uncle Ed's house.

"We own 300 acres of the best woods this side of the Mississippi. It provides us with all we need. We take good care of her and she takes good care of us," said Uncle Ed.

He added," Today we're going to cut wood on Rembrandt's Ridge. There are some big trees that fell this fall and we need them for the stove," he said.

I could see a road cut through the woods. As soon as we stepped into the woods, it was like I had stepped back in time. I looked around and noticed all the maple trees had been tapped. There were tubes coming out into small buckets even though it wasn't sap season right now. The operation looked interesting.

Uncle Ed was in his glory as we walked. He told me stories of how they bought the land over thirty years ago. He retired ten years earlier from the County Road Commission and had built a sap shack to make homemade maple syrup. Every spring he looked forward to sap season.

After walking for a while, I stopped. Something to the west had caught my eye.

"Uncle Ed, what's over there?" I asked pointing down the ridge.

There looked to be an opening of some sort, like there was once a road or trail running through the woods.

Uncle Ed turned to see where I was pointing. Instantly his demeanor changed and he got a menacing look on his face.

"That's the West Woods. You aren't ever allowed to go there!" he said.

Ever!

- 15 -

There was something really strange about the way Uncle Ed acted when I pointed at the mysterious lane leading into the West Woods. It was kind of hidden from view, so I could only see it as we walked up the ridge, but something was there.

Judging by Uncle Ed's response, it was probably a place I didn't belong.

"Come on, we're almost there," Uncle Ed said returning to his cheerful self.

After about ten more minutes of walking, we came to an open spot. There were several huge trees laying on the ground and piles of firewood stacked neatly.

He must have spent hours back in this area cutting wood.

"I'll cut; you stack," he yelled as he pulled the

cord on the chainsaw. The loud blaring sound of the chainsaw was soothing in a way because it helped drown out my thoughts.

For the next five hours we worked hard. I actually liked working in the woods with Uncle Ed. Even though it was my first day, I felt stronger, like I was accomplishing something.

Around noon, Uncle Ed put the chainsaw down.

"Let's eat," he said reaching into his backpack and pulling out leftovers from the night before. It seemed like I was always hungry here, but I was especially hungry after cutting wood.

"Just something about a good hard day's work, it does something for the soul," Uncle Ed said.

He was right.

I looked around munching on an apple from Aunt Loretta's famous orchard. The crisp skin snapped in my mouth as I bit into it. The late October air was cold enough for me to see my breath. I wasn't sure but I would guess temperatures were cold enough for snow.

I sat on a log enjoying my lunch when a sudden movement caught my eye. I squinted and could see something moving down the ridge near the creek. It was a deer; and not just that, it was a buck!

I hadn't seen a lot of deer in my life. In fact, besides the ones we saw on the ride up from Detroit, this was one of the first deer I had ever seen in the wild.

"Uncle Ed, look at that!" I whispered.

The buck crept along the creek and had a magnificent 6-point rack. Uncle Ed could see the look of amazement on my face.

"Pretty neat. Have you ever deer hunted before?" he asked.

"No, but I'd love to," I quickly shot back.

Uncle Ed looked at me with a sly grin.

"I have a crossbow you can use. We can practice later today and see if you like shooting it. If you do, I'll take you to town and get a license. I have lots of tree stands just waiting for someone to shoot a buck from," said Uncle Ed with a grin.

Back in Detroit, I was part of an afterschool program that taught us about nature and the outdoors. Part of the class was taking the hunter safety course, so I had already taken it and passed.

I could barely contain myself. I never moved quicker and stacked wood so fast. The rest of the afternoon flew by. I couldn't wait to shoot his crossbow.

Something inside me stirred because I had always wanted to go deer hunting. After seeing that buck walking along the creek, I could barely contain myself.

~ 16 ~

We finally finished cutting wood around 4:00 and started walking back towards the house. This time Uncle Ed walked on my right side. I wasn't sure why, but it seemed like he was trying to hide something.

When we got back to the house, I quickly got cleaned up. I couldn't wait to shoot Uncle Ed's crossbow.

The smell of homemade sweet potatoes and a honey-cured ham filled the tiny house.

"Uncle Ed is going to let me shoot his crossbow," I said excitedly.

"You do have an hour until supper is done, so go ahead," she said with a smile.

I took off out of the house and saw Uncle Ed walking out of the barn with his crossbow. It was black and looked cool, but it wasn't as heavy as I thought it would be. Uncle Ed gave me a safety lesson and some shooting pointers.

"Hold steady and squeeze the trigger, be surprised when it goes off," he told me as I shouldered the crossbow.

It was a weird feeling, I was nervous yet excited. My first shot hit the target! I was amazed at the speed the arrow had. I shot again and this time it was a bullseye!

We stayed and shot for another 20 minutes. By the time we were done, I felt really confident with his crossbow.

"Am I ready, can I hunt now?" I asked.

"Almost," Uncle Ed said with a smile. He walked over and took the crossbow from me. He put it away and motioned for me to get in his truck.

"We need to get you a hunting license so you're legal. There's just enough time before dinner to go get one from Nolde's Hardware," he said.

On the drive to Nolde's I started to ask Uncle Ed a lot of questions about hunting. He told me about the best places to hunt in his woods and what to look for.

When we finally pulled into the hardware store, I almost didn't want to get out because I was so enjoying listening to his hunting stories. We both went in and within minutes were back in the truck, license in hand. I had everything I needed to go into the woods after my first buck.

At least that's what I thought.

~ 17 ~

As soon as we got back home, we sat down and had dinner. It was amazing as usual. I think Aunt Loretta could have cooked anything well—everything she made tasted amazing. Over the last couple of months I had eaten a lot of fast food, and after the divorce, we seldom sat down and ate together.

"So Uncle Ed, can I hunt tomorrow morning?" I finally asked when he was done with most of his food.

"Nope. Sorry Tucker, can't hunt in the morning. Tomorrow is Sunday, and we never miss church," Uncle Ed said.

My mom went to church on most Sundays. It seemed like she went more often after the divorce, but I usually didn't go with her.

"But I got a perfect spot for you tomorrow

night," he said with a wink. His response brought me instant joy. I knew Uncle Ed would know where we needed to be to get a buck.

Even though I had only been there 24 hours, I was starting to like country living. I felt good after a hard day's work, way better than all the late nights and days I slept in.

That night, however, I barely slept. I kept picturing that six-point buck. I think I was having the early stages of buck fever. It seemed like I had just fallen asleep when I felt a tug on my arm. Uncle Ed was standing there smiling; it was already morning.

"I let you sleep in, but now it's time to get up," said Uncle Ed. I rolled over and saw my alarm clock read 6:00. I got up and Aunt Loretta had breakfast ready. It was still dark as I glanced out at the October moon.

"Going to be a good night to be in the woods. A cold front is moving in and the deer will be moving," Uncle Ed said.

"Is that good for deer?" I asked, not knowing much about hunting.

"The next couple weeks are the best time to be in the woods," said Uncle Ed.

That got me even more excited. I scarfed down my breakfast and headed to the barn to start morning chores. Uncle Ed had a small hobby farm. He had a couple cows, chickens, and pigs. We worked for about an hour cleaning out their pens and getting them fresh water.

I liked to watch Uncle Ed work with his animals. He talked to them like they were his own kids, like they were a part of his family.

"You can tell a lot about a person by the way they treat their animals," he said.

Time flew by quickly and soon Aunt Loretta yelled from the back porch, "Boys, you need to wash up and get ready for church!" Without missing a beat, Uncle Ed hung up his watering pail and walked into the house. I followed, trying to learn everything as quickly as possible.

I jumped in the shower and washed up. As I was drying off a scary thought hit me. I didn't have any fancy, dress clothes. I just packed jeans, jogging pants, and school clothes. I didn't think my boring black shirt was going to be appropriate for church.

But to my surprise, there laying on the bed was a pair of dress pants, collared shirt, and tie. I wanted to ask them where they got the clothes but didn't want to look ungrateful.

The three of us loaded up in Uncle Ed's truck and motored down the road to church, just one big happy family.

They attended Wilderness Valley Christian Church. It was a small church with about forty people, and everyone seemed kind and genuine. They introduced me to some of the congregation and some kids that I would be going to school with. I smiled and acted interested but really wasn't. The only thing I could think about was getting in the woods that night to hunt for the first time.

I felt happy sitting in a pew between Uncle Ed and Aunt Loretta. I listened to the preacher and enjoyed his sermon. As soon as church was over, I ran for the truck. It took Uncle Ed and Aunt Loretta a couple minutes to come out.

"Are you a little excited?" asked Uncle Ed.

"Just a little," I replied.

"Don't worry, we'll get you in the woods soon," Uncle Ed said with a grin.

~ 18 ~

We got home and had a light lunch. It was about 1:00 when we finally got around to hunting. Uncle Ed had some extra camouflage for me to wear.

I laughed as I put it on. The kids at Washington Carver Middle School would have gotten a good laugh at the great Tucker in camo three times his size.

We started hiking back into the woods, down the same trail we used to cut wood. We stopped about halfway back. I was amazed at how good Uncle Ed could still move for an old guy.

"Okay, Tucker. The stand you are going to hunt from is right there at the top of that ridge. You're going to be sitting over a cut corn field. It's a great spot," he said.

I turned to look back and noticed this time

Uncle Ed was sending me east; he was going to do anything to keep me from the West Woods.

"Tucker, are you listening?" asked Uncle Ed.

"Sorry," I said as I turned back around.

"You're going to walk up that ridge and sit in the tree stand," said Uncle Ed.

He quickly added, "Whatever you do, don't get up and walk around. I'll be waiting for you right here when it gets dark." I nodded. I understood the plan. Sit in the tree stand, wait until dark, and meet him back here.

"Shoot straight," he said as he turned and walked back towards the house.

I walked up the ridge and found a ladder stand overlooking the corn field just like Uncle Ed had said. I climbed the ladder and got ready. I didn't see anything for the first couple of hours but then deer starting filing into the corn field from every direction.

I felt like a warrior perched for battle. I was really enjoying being in the outdoors. This was something I could never have imagined doing when we were living in Detroit.

A flock of geese flew overhead; their honking made a noisy fall quartet. I was still amazed at just how gorgeous fall was in the Upper Peninsula, both the sights and sounds. It was like something out of a dream.

The sound of a twig breaking brought me back to reality. I turned and slowly looked over my left shoulder. I couldn't believe my eyes! It was that six-point buck from earlier and he was close.

Suddenly I started to shake and my knees felt weak. I didn't know what was happening. I thought I was having a heart attack. My whole body trembled and I could barely function. I picked up the crossbow and had to put it down. I was shaking so bad I couldn't hold it still.

I tried to calm myself, but every time I looked up, I saw his white rack coming closer and closer. I couldn't believe it—my very first hunt and I was about to get my first buck.

The closer the buck got, the more I shook. I pulled up the crossbow and the buck looked even bigger in the scope!

I thought my heart was going to jump out of my chest.

I took aim and tried to steady the crosshairs on the buck. He was close, only about twenty yards away.

The crosshairs danced on his brown hide as I quickly jerked the trigger.

I watched the arrow land five feet in front of the buck and the entire field emptied back into the woods.

I had missed!

- 19 -

I was devastated, I had a chance to get a buck and missed. I started looking and noticed a branch was broken in front of me.

My arrow must've hit something. I was so disappointed, I thought about getting down but figured I still had a couple hours of light left. Plus, I found hunting to be peaceful and relaxing even though I had missed that buck.

There was something special about Uncle Ed's woods; maybe it was just being in the outdoors. It was strange to describe, but the woods had a mystical quality.

Sitting in the tree stand allowed me to think. It was the first time I actually thought about my parents and what had happened at school.

I felt bad I didn't even tell my dad goodbye. He called last night but I told Uncle Ed I didn't want to talk to him. I had already talked to my mom twice since arriving at Uncle Ed's house. She was busy with Tina and seemed relieved that I was out of the house.

The divorce affected me even more than I had known. Everything had changed so fast, I didn't have time to adjust. Most of my anger was towards my dad, but really I was upset with both of them. I thought our family meant more to them than that. I couldn't believe how easy it seemed for them to just give up.

Various memories rolled through my mind. The peacefulness of hunting was something I had never experienced. For the first time since the divorce, I had time to clear my head and think.

Why did they get divorced? I wondered. *Was it money? Someone else? Was it me?*

The sun was starting to go down and I looked back over my shoulder to the spot where Uncle Ed had told me to meet him. I wanted to make sure I knew exactly how to get there. Even though I had a flashlight, everything was new to me.

As I was turning around, I saw movement to

my left. I saw a little white flicker—it was a tail! There was a doe walking my way, followed by a buck. This one was even bigger than the one I missed. I counted 8-points!

Then the shaking started again. I realized I wasn't going to die, I had buck fever!

The buck was walking a different path than the first one but was going to end up in the field right in front of me.

This time I looked for a clear shot through the trees. I peered through the scope and found an opening in the brush. This time I imagined myself on the mound in the bottom of the ninth inning. I calmed my nerves and slowly pulled the trigger.

Whack! I watched the arrow blast through the buck. I had hit my first buck! The deer spun and ran west towards the trail I had walked in on.

I exhaled slowly, my legs were shaking so badly I couldn't stand up. I have never before felt that kind of excitement in my life.

It was just starting to get dark but I couldn't wait any longer. I had to see if I got that buck.

What would 10 minutes hurt to get down a little early. I crawled down the ladder stand. Uncle Ed had told me to wait until dark and he would come and get me.

I could see the arrow sticking in the ground. The fletching was covered in blood, and I thought I had a good hit. I followed drops of blood as they weaved through the woods back to the trail.

"I'll just track it a little while and stop," I told myself.

I continued down the ridge following the blood trail; it was easy because there were large spots of blood on the fallen leaves.

I was so excited when I hit the trail; I kept my head down and kept tracking west. It was getting dark fast but I didn't notice it because I was consumed with finding my buck.

After ten minutes, I stopped and looked around. It was dark and I had wandered deep in the West Woods, well past the end mark of the trail that Uncle Ed had set. I had gotten caught up in tracking and now was lost in the West Woods. My hands were numb and my heart sank.

~ 20 ~

I looked in every direction, but all I could see were the towering trunks from the ancient trees that populated Uncle Ed's property. I had been so focused on looking for my deer, I had no idea when or where I turned.

I stopped and leaned against a nearby tree. I had to gather my thoughts and make a plan to rescue myself. I unzipped my backpack and pulled out a flashlight. I turned it on, but it didn't help much. It was so dark under the canopy of the forest, the flashlight gave me little light, just enough to see about three feet in every direction.

I felt like I was going to get sick, my stomach tossed and turned. I had light but had no idea in what direction to go. I had gotten turned around in the woods and lost all sense of direction.

I began walking along the ridge line. I had

gone pretty far and still had no idea where the trail was. I started to panic and shone my light in all directions, hoping to find a landmark or something that looked familiar.

Then the flashlight went out. I quickly shook it and the light faintly came back on. I knew I didn't have much time left before the light would be completely dead. Just then, my light hit something and reflected. At first it was hard to see but I could see it was something manmade. I squinted, trying to read what was written on the sign as my light blinked on and off.

I walked closer, squinting trying to read what was written on the sign. I wiped my hand across it to clean off the mud that had helped camouflage it against the tree.

DANGER: DO NOT ENTER was written in an eerie red. The paint had run and dried, making it look like it was written in blood. As soon as I read the last word, the light went out. I hit the flashlight as hard as I could and shook it, but nothing happened. I was deeper in the woods and more lost then I could have ever imagined.

I sat down and clutched the sign. I was drawn to it; there was something mysterious about it. I was lost in thought. My head was down and my eyes closed for a second. When I opened them, I saw a small yellowish glow beneath my feet. My light had turned back on.

I aimed it towards where the sign had hung and could make out what appeared to be an entrance to an old road. All the grass had grown up, but it was obvious something had been there.

I took a couple steps down the path as the light continued to flicker. There was something in the distance and it was big. I couldn't tell what it was, but it appeared to be some type of building. That was all I could make out as the light died out one last time.

I stood in complete darkness feeling around for a nearby tree. I was tired from tracking my deer. My mind was racing. *What were those buildings for? Why did Uncle Ed not tell me about them? What was he trying to protect?*

The temperature was dropping and it was starting to get cold. I decided to take a minute, close my eyes, and clear my head. My legs enjoyed the break and my mind started to wander. I knew it wasn't a good idea, but I couldn't fight it. I was worn out from traveling, from getting up so early, and from cutting wood. After a couple minutes, I caught myself starting to nod off. I fought the feeling several times, but my eyelids gave in.

My body went warm; at first I thought I was dead. I had heard on television that you get a warm sensation when you die. I always wondered how they knew that since dead people don't talk.

In my dream I was in a good place. I was on the baseball diamond. It was a warm summer day and I could see kids playing and laughing. I looked over and saw my dad clapping and giving high fives.

I knew where I was. It was two summers ago. It was one of my greatest memories; we were playing in the city league championship and I was pitching. Dad was so proud of me that day. I struck out twelve batters and our team won by two runs. I watched Mom and Dad interact, smiling at each other. The sun beamed on my face, I could feel the warmth; the happiness felt so real.

Then my dream was interrupted by a frantic scream. At first I was mad, I didn't want to leave the ball fields. This was the last time we would all be together; the last time I was happy.

The screams were getting louder and closer pulling me off the baseball diamond.

~ 21 ~

Tucker! Tucker!

I jerked awake and found myself propped against a white pine, still somewhere in the West Woods. I scowled as I quickly realized my dream was gone and I was back in my nightmare.

It was Uncle Ed's voice, and even though it was dark I could see a small glow over one of the nearby hills.

I almost yelled back but stopped myself. I didn't want him to know what I found, I knew he would be angry. He might even have my dad come and get me. I had found his secret, something he wanted to hide from me.

But why? It didn't matter now, the only thing that mattered was getting out of the woods without Uncle Ed knowing what I had found.

Reaching out, I used my hands and feet to

guide me and started towards Uncle Ed's dim light. After about ten minutes, I let out a yell.

"Here," I yelled. He quickly responded and I saw the light working its way to me. I couldn't help but wonder in the back of my mind if he was concerned about me or worried I had found his secret.

He walked up and hugged me.

"Tucker, I was worried sick!" he said. I was relieved. I could tell in his tone that he was genuine. I had learned not to trust people so it was refreshing to know someone was worried about me, someone actually missed me.

I quickly told him about the buck and how I was tracking it when my light died.

"How far west did you track it?" he asked. His voice was different; it was still worried but there was something else on his mind.

"Oh not far, my light died almost right away," I said. He wasn't convinced.

"How far did you go?" he asked again.

"I don't even know, Uncle Ed, all I saw was trees. I was lost. I couldn't even tell you where I was," I said. I wasn't lying. I didn't want to tell him what I saw, at least not yet.

I tried acting so excited about my buck to take Uncle Ed's mind off the West Woods.

"Okay, these woods can be dangerous if you wander off. Let's get you back to the house. I'll come out in the morning while you're at school and find your buck," said Uncle Ed.

I was excited to see my buck but could tell he didn't want me to go into the woods without him. He wanted to find it, but more than anything he wanted me to stay away from his secret.

We were welcomed back to the house by a warm supper from Aunt Loretta. She had made a venison roast, potatoes, and asparagus.

After dinner, I did some reading and headed to bed. I couldn't get what I saw out of my mind. I had a roller coaster of emotions. First the excitement of shooting my first buck, then the mystery of all the buildings in the middle of the woods, and finally the fear of Uncle Ed knowing what I saw.

Was it an old moonshine operation? Did

Uncle Ed rob a bank and stash money there? By the time I fell asleep, I had convinced myself he was one of Al Capone's gangsters.

The next morning it wasn't my ears that woke me up, it was my nose. There was a strong smell coming from the kitchen. The aroma of onions, ground beef, and seasoned pork filled the air, providing the best alarm clock.

I peeked out and could see Aunt Loretta rolling dough and making what looked like little pies.

"What's for breakfast?" I asked, strolling over and putting my hands on her shoulders.

"Pasties, my dear. Sit down. You are about to have a real Yooper treat," she said.

I plopped down at the kitchen table and Aunt Loretta walked over with two fresh pasties. I took a big bite and proceeded to wolf down both of them. The taste was unreal; I couldn't believe how good they were.

"Where's Uncle Ed?" I asked.

"He got up early to go get your buck," she said.

I knew he was excited about finding my first buck. I had to know more about that hidden place in the West Woods.

"Aunt Loretta, can I ask you something?" I said.

"Sure honey, you can ask your old Auntie anything," she said. She was gentle, and her voice was always thoughtful.

"It's about the West Woods. The place Uncle Ed doesn't want me to go," I asked.

She turned and looked at me, with a look of concern.

What was it about this place?

Just then Uncle Ed walked in. Aunt Loretta stopped just as she was about to say something.

"I found him—a nice 8-point. Great job, Tucker!"

I was excited and ran outside to see it. Uncle Ed had my buck hanging from the rafters in the barn. It was so big! I was proud of myself. I never thought I would like to hunt, but I loved it.

"You better get your things, the bus will be here soon," Uncle Ed said.

I rushed back into the house to grab my book bag.

I threw on my jacket and gave Aunt Loretta a kiss on her cheek.

"You might need a good book to read at school," she whispered.

I stopped. I wasn't sure what she was talking about. I wasn't much of a reader and there were lots of books at the school library. She could tell I was confused.

She added," Why don't you go pick out a good book from our library, one that looks interesting."

Still confused, I walked into the den where the small library was. There were about 100 books on all kinds of subjects, but one instantly caught my eye. It was leather bound, making it stand out from the other books. I walked over and pulled it off the shelf.

It was some type of old journal. I wiped the dust off the front. The pages were yellow and weathered. For some strange reason I knew that this was the book Aunt Loretta was hinting at me to read.

The Adventures of the Tall Tale Deer Camp

"Where the bucks are big,
but the stories are bigger."

Seemed interesting to me. I gave it a quick glance and threw it in my book bag as I rushed out the door.

~ 22 ~

I stared out the window as the yellow school bus rumbled down the dusty back roads, picking up Plainville students. I waited a couple of minutes to make sure no one was going to sit with me.

As I opened the book, the pages creaked to life.

November 14, 1971

It's finally here! We have waited all year for the opener and it should be a good one. J.D. brought Mickey and Tom. Me, Big Bob, Otis, and Preacher met them at the cabin around 7:30 p.m. There's a little bit of snow on the ground. We found a huge track coming back to camp, hoping it's old Bullwinkle. He's a legend around here, might be a 20-point buck but not really sure since none of us has ever seen him. But there sure are a lot of stories about the old buck. This is the first year for camp, so glad Loretta and I bought the old Hitchcock place. We're going to have eleven days of food, cards, and big bucks at the Tall Tale Deer Camp. There's just something magical about deer camp and the opening day of deer season in the U.P.

—Ed

Wow! This was dated over thirty years ago, so Uncle Ed would have been around 40 years old.

The idea of a bunch of people staying out in the woods chasing deer seemed kind of funny at first. But there was something about it, about the way it was written. This was something that these guys were so passionate about. I had to keep reading.

November 15, 1971

Otis missed a big one! That poor boy has terrible luck. Ed and I both sat near the West Woods, hoping for Bullwinkle but had no luck. I shot a big doe around 10:30 a.m. It took all our strength for Ed and me to drag her up the ridge, but she'll be good eating back at camp. The sun peered over the ridge, and it was the most glorious picture God ever created. I'm so glad Ed and Loretta brought us all up here, it's a good break for me from the season. I fly back out tomorrow but two days of deer camp is better than no days at deer camp.

—J.D.

Who is J.D.? I wonder where he is now.

The bus screeched to a halt as we arrived at high school. I didn't want to get off, but when Mr. Mark, the bus driver, hollered my name, I knew I had to go inside school. I slipped the journal into my bag but couldn't take my mind off it. When the bell finally rang at 3:00, I rushed back to the bus. I had to read more—I was hooked.

November 18, 1971

It was sad seeing J.D. leave, but we understand. We were just thankful to have him for the

*time we did. I have been praying every morning
that Mickey sees a deer, I am sick of hearing him
whine. So far Otis and I are the Euchre champs,
but we play Big Bob and Tom tonight. The food
has been fabulous; we are so thankful for
Loretta's world famous pasties. Life is great, so
far the first year of the Tall Tale Deer Camp is a
huge success. The boys are already talking about
adding another building to eat in and play cards,
I guess we have already outgrown the two cab-
ins.*

— Preacher

November 25, 1971

*We're starting to pack up, what a sad day. The
last eleven days have been some of the best days
of my life. Otis ended up getting a nice 4-point
and Tom shot a spike on the last day. Two bucks
and four does total, not bad for our first camp.
We're hoping next year J.D. can stay longer and
one of us runs into Bullwinkle. Otis claims he
saw him this morning, but none of us believe him.
Although the leaves are gone, the Upper*

Peninsula of Michigan is still one of the most beautiful places on earth in November. I think I'll be able to still hear the laughs and card games until next year.

—Ed

Even though I had just started reading the journal, one thing was clear—I wish I could have been part of the Tall Tale Deer Camp.

I got off the bus and walked into the house. I kept the journal in my school backpack; I wasn't ready to bring it up to Uncle Ed.

"Hey, honey," Aunt Loretta called from the kitchen.

She was doing dishes and Uncle Ed was at the table. She winked at me, somehow she knew I had found the book. There was fresh cornbread sitting on the table with some homemade strawberry jam. I sat down and started eating.

"What's that?" Uncle Ed asked pointing to my book bag. I had forgotten to zip up my backpack, and there sitting out in plain sight was the journal.

"What is that?" he asked again pointing towards the opening in my backpack.

~ 23 ~

I was searching for a way out and didn't know what to say. I looked at Aunt Loretta but she just shrugged her shoulders.

"Is that your history book?" he asked.

I looked at my bag and quickly grabbed my tattered history book that was sitting below the journal.

"Yeah, this is my *World History* book," I said.

"I love history, you mind if I look at it?" he asked.

"Sure," I said as I handed him the book. Whew! He hadn't noticed the journal. Uncle Ed skimmed through the book, highlighting some of his favorite historical events. I listened to him tell me about World War II and the collapse of the Roman Empire.

"I got homework, do you mind if I go into my

room and work on it? You can keep the book, I have other subjects to study," I said. I wasn't lying, but there was only one thing I planned on studying that night,

"That a boy, you go study. You can learn a lot from books," Uncle Ed said.

"You sure can," piped in Aunt Loretta as she walked back into the kitchen.

I went to my room, sat down on the bed, and pulled out the brown leather journal.

November 14, 1972

I thought deer camp would never come. We had a busy summer at Tall Tale Camp; we added two more buildings. The recreation room is serving as dining room and Euchre headquarters. We also added a small cabin we plan on using for camp member meetings and church. Preacher was happy to have a place up here, and we made it a rule that every member had to attend church on Sunday, even during deer camp. That makes four buildings, eight guys, and hopefully lots of big bucks. J.D. is the only one not here, due to work, but he hopes to make it the last week of camp. Otis still swears he saw Bullwinkle on his drive into camp. We just joked that he was delirious from the drive from Chicago. The guys came from all over, but they said they wouldn't miss deer camp for anything. I'm looking forward to the next couple weeks. I love a lot of holidays, but there are none more exciting than November 15, the opening day of gun season in Michigan at Tall Tale Deer Camp.

—Ed

November 15, 1972
Tom missed a nice 10-point buck. Otis fell asleep and didn't see anything. Mickey shot at a doe and we're going to track it after dark, I hope he hit her good; we need meat for camp. I saw three deer but they were too far away. Today was such a joy as I rejoiced and gave thanks to God for deer camp.

—Preacher

November 17, 1972

What a great couple of days! Tale Tall Deer Camp is booming; we have added a couple new members. We have 13 guys that are part of camp. The hunting has been slow—one buck, a 9-point was killed by Steve Freeman. Steve is a principal and has known Preacher for years. I'm glad he got a buck. He drove all the way up from Saginaw just to hunt. Otis claims he saw Bullwinkle last night near the beaver pond, but it was too late to shoot. I think Otis sees things, not sure if Bullwinkle even exists. J.D. made it in today, now camp is complete. He's sore from the game but ready to hunt and play cards. It seems like the 11 days spent at deer camp go by too fast. I sat in my blind all day. I took a couple naps and read the entire November edition of Woods-N-Water Magazine.

—Ed

November 18, 1972

Mickey finally shot a buck, a wide 11-pointer. It's not Bullwinkle, but it's by far the biggest

buck we have gotten at Tall Tale Deer Camp.
J.D. missed a four-point, and he's stuck cleaning
out the bathroom. He was thrilled.

—Otis

Page after page, I couldn't put it down. I could see why Tall Tale Deer Camp was so popular, a fall rite of passage for these men. I wanted to be there; I wanted a place to go to like that, somewhere to forget about all my problems and enjoy fellowship.

The stories kept spilling out of the pages, one adventure after another. I kept reading, year after year, the adventures, the tales told about Tall Tale Deer Camp intrigued me.

For the next two weeks, I read the journal every night before bed. I tucked the book under my pillow. The book was thick; it reminded me of the Bible. At first I thought I would never read the entire book.

Slowly I chipped away, I was six years into the camp journal. There were many changes around the deer camp. New buildings went up, some members left and new ones were added. It was quite the operation. One thing that never changed was the original seven members: Uncle Ed, J.D., Preacher, Mickey, Tom, Bob, and Otis. They were best friends; they were like brothers. Hunting, eating, and having fun was a constant throughout the journal. The goal was the same every year— try to bag Bullwinkle. I finally caught on, every big buck around camp automatically got the nickname Bullwinkle.

The thought of a deer camp, a place to retreat to, seemed so special. There were lots of stories, but even more references to all the fun they had.

The once meaty book was now down to only a couple pages. I was sad since I didn't want the book to end. I was hoping there was a second book, one just as thick and full of adventures.

I heard a knock on the door and quickly threw the journal under my pillow. It was Uncle Ed. I had really grown to respect and admire my Uncle Ed and Aunt Loretta over the past month. They were honest, loving, and patient. I wondered why they didn't have any kids of their own because they would have been great parents.

"I just wanted to say goodnight. I also wanted to tell you how much your aunt and I are enjoying having you around," said Uncle Ed.

It was nice to have someone want me around, to notice me.

"Thanks, Uncle Ed. I'm enjoying it, I really like hunting, and I really like Plainsville," I said.

He smiled.

"I knew you would, I wish everyone from the city could come up and spend some time in the U.P. I think it would solve a lot of the world's problems," he said.

I nodded.

It was the first week of November and gun season was right around the corner.

"Can you take me gun hunting?" I asked.

"I don't gun hunt anymore, Tucker," said Uncle Ed. "I prefer to stay out of the woods when all the gun hunters move in, that's why I bow hunt. I haven't gun hunted in years."

He could tell I was disappointed. After reading about all the excitement of November 15, gun season in the U.P. was something I wanted to experience.

"No big deal, I already got my buck anyway," I said with a smile.

Uncle Ed grinned and walked out.

"Leave the light on, I have a little more reading tonight," I said.

The door shut and I opened up the journal and saw there were only two pages left.

I had to see how it all ended, what happened to the Tall Tale Deer Camp.

I sat reflecting, how could something this great just end? What could possibly have happened?

I was about to find out.

- 24 -

November 14, 1977

Another year and even more excitement around camp. We actually saw a giant buck during some pre-season scouting. We think it might be Bullwinkle. This buck is the biggest anyone has ever seen, and it will make the hunter who bags him a famous man.

J.D. doesn't think he will make camp as his team is chasing a playoff berth. We'll have to wait and see what happens. Preacher plans on winning our Opening Night Chili Cook-Off. It would be three years in a row if he does. Some think he gets the most votes because he's a Pastor, but I think it's because his wife helps him make his chili. As I sit and write, I can hear the laughs and stories at camp. There are about twenty guys here, waiting for tomorrow morning.

We got pasties, homemade jerky, and tons of junk food.

Thank God for deer camp!

—Ed

Something major has to happen; there was only one page left.

I flipped to the next page and saw three short entries.

November 18, 1977

Bullwinkle was officially spotted by two hunters along the north ridge heading west. No shots, but all the stories have everyone excited. So far, four bucks and five does have been taken. J.D. flew in today; we were all surprised and happy to see him, even though he seemed a little grumpy.

—Otis

November 19, 1977

More sightings of Bullwinkle. I know where to find him. He was seen crossing Old Man's thicket near the west end of the property. I have hunted here long enough to know, Bullwinkle is living in Zeppelin's Swamp. I know just the stand to sit in. He'll be mine tomorrow.

—Ed

November 20, 1977

Ugly day, the worst day in the history of Tall Tale Deer Camp. Bullwinkle is dead—what a trophy! The buck is a record book caliber buck with 14-scorable points, and his thick palmated horns make him even more unique.

The problem is both Ed and J.D. shot him. It's getting ugly; both men are adamant that it's their buck. We had to break them up as they almost started a fist fight. J.D. said some things he shouldn't have and Ed had enough. This is bad...

—Otis

November 21, 1977

A bunch of guys left camp early. It got really bad with guys taking sides over the Bullwinkle buck, while most felt it should be Ed's, J.D. had some guys that joined him.

There was a lot of yelling. This is the first time camp has ever ended early. It's also the first time I saw Ed so mad; he told everyone to get off his property. Hopefully, this will pass. There will always be a piece of me at Tall Tale Deer Camp.
—Preacher

An argument over a buck? That is what ended Tall Tale? Uncle Ed and J.D. got in a fight over who killed Bullwinkle?

I made up my mind. I had to see Tall Tale Deer Camp with my own eyes. I had to go back to the forbidden spot in Uncle Ed's woods, the place where I had discovered all the buildings. Now I knew why Uncle Ed wanted to keep me out of part of the woods—he didn't want me to see the camp. He knew I would ask questions. He would have to relive it.

I had no choice, I had to see the camp during the daytime.

~ 25 ~

I wanted to ask Uncle Ed but knew he didn't want to talk about it. Since my first day, he had done everything to keep me from this place, to keep his secret buried. He wanted it to stay hidden, to stay lost.

The next day school seemed to last forever, I thought the bell would never ring. I was so excited to get home, go back, and find the camp. I already had a mental picture of what the camp looked like after reading in the journal.

I stared out the window as Bus 97 trucked down the road. As the bus came to a stop, I could see Uncle Ed's truck was missing from the driveway. I sprinted into the house.

"Slow down, Tucker, there isn't a fire," said Aunt Loretta with a smile. I caught my breath near the kitchen table.

"Where's Uncle Ed?" I managed to force out between heavy breaths.

"I sent him to the store; he should be back in about an hour," she said with a wink. I wasn't going to ask, but it was almost like Aunt Loretta wanted to help me in my quest, like she knew exactly what I was doing and wanted me to do it.

I kissed her cheek and ran out the back door. I knew right where to go. It took me about 15 minutes to reach the back spot where I had walked out to meet Uncle Ed the night I shot my buck. From there, I knew I had to walk west.

The more I walked, the rougher the terrain was. I stopped and looked around for a smoother path. I saw an opening to my left and walked over to the road, although it wasn't really a road anymore. I looked forward and back and saw there was a clear change in vegetation. I was walking down the road that brought all the hunters to Tall Tale Deer Camp. After ten more minutes of walking, I saw the old beat up sign. It wasn't as scary as it had been when I came face to face with it in the dark.

The blood color was obviously some old red paint, and I could tell by the handwriting it was Uncle Ed's. I started ripping down vines and brush. It was thick and I had to fight to get through the next fifty yards of woods.

Then it opened up and I got a full view of Tall Tale Deer Camp. Even with all its age, the camp was majestic!

It looked like it was its own small town. I jogged towards it. In the center was a huge campfire area with benches that looked like an outdoor theater. I sat down and closed my eyes. I could only imagine all the great stories told around the fire.

After imagining for a minute, I got up and walked towards the main building in the middle. There was a big yellow KEEP OUT sign above the door. I reached up and pulled it off, revealing the words BUNKHOUSE. I knew this from the journal and opened the old pine door. There, still intact, stood twelve bunk beds. The beds still had their sheets on them and looked like someone had just spend the weekend.

I walked out and explored the other six buildings. Tall Tale was like its own small town. Every building had a name carved above the door. Church was filled with six pews and even had a pulpit. This is where Preacher held Sunday service on both Sundays during the 11-day deer camp.

The recreation room was still decorated with deer heads and card tables. Playing cards were still on most of the tables along with wooden colored chips. If I hadn't known better, I would think everyone left suddenly because of some danger like a tornado. Everything was still in place, like that day in 1977 when the camp ended.

I couldn't get over how clean everything was for being abandoned for the last thirty years. It was like it was sitting, waiting for all its campers to come back for one more deer camp.

I was lost in thought when I heard a loud creak. I turned to see a shadow standing in the doorway.

"What are you doing here?" demanded an angry voice out of the darkness. It was Uncle Ed.

~ 26 ~

Uncle Ed's face was bright red. There was nowhere to go, I had to talk to him about the camp.

I was sick of running. It seemed like for the past six months running was all I'd done. Running from school to school, running from my parents' divorce, and running from myself. I was done running.

"Sorry, Uncle Ed. I just had to see it, I had to see Tale Tall Deer Camp for myself," I said.

The bright red color left Uncle Ed's face and he let out a soft sigh.

"Tall Tale Deer Camp, I haven't heard that in a while," he said almost with a sense of relief.

"What a glorious place, I couldn't stop myself, not after reading all about it. I just had to see it, just one time," I said.

"I knew I should have thrown out that old journal," said Uncle Ed.

He quickly added, "I just couldn't though. There was a part of me that didn't want to forget. I knew as long as I kept that old book, this place would still be real."

We walked over and sat down at a nearby table. Uncle Ed could tell I was confused. He had been trying to hide this place for all those years, but his voice was full of love. To Uncle Ed, this place was like Camelot or Atlantis—something that was sacred.

I looked around. There were no spiderwebs, no damage to anything inside. The camp looked strange but not how I expected. I thought thirty years would have taken its toll on the camp. But it hadn't. The camp was for the most part in great condition.

It looked like someone took a picture, and it stayed the exact same since that day so long ago. I reached down and wiped the table—no dust. Uncle Ed could tell I had a lot of questions.

"I couldn't ever really leave this place—too

many laughs, too many memories," he said quietly.

He added, "I come out about once a month and keep the place clean. We put a lot of love into this camp; I just couldn't watch her die."

For over thirty years Uncle Ed had been making the trek back into the woods to clean and take care of Tall Tale Camp.

Why didn't he just keep the camp going? I could tell by the why he talked, this was his favorite place on earth.

"What happened? Why would anyone ever stop coming, why did Tall Tale Deer Camp close if you loved it this much?" I asked.

He looked up at me with a sad look.

"They didn't stop coming; I did," he said.

Uncle Ed started to tear up and looked out the window.

"It was all over a buck," he said.

The journal had talked about how getting this big buck would be one for the record books.

"How can a deer ruin this?" I asked looking around the camp.

"It was huge, a buck of a lifetime. Everyone wanted him. He was supposed to hang above the fireplace in here," he said pointing over to the east wall.

"I shot him first, put a real good hit on him. He was a bruiser; he kept going though. He ended up going another couple hundred yards and walked right in front of J.D. He pulled up and put the finishing shot in him," said Uncle Ed.

"What happened next was a nightmare. I ran over all excited, only to have J.D. sitting on top guarding the giant buck. He told me it was his trophy, and we got into a big, messy argument. We were so loud other hunters came over to see what the fuss was all about. People starting taking sides and it got ugly," said Uncle Ed as he rubbed his head.

He added, "I lost my cool. I kicked everyone out of camp, told them I was calling the cops and would have them arrested if they didn't leave. J.D. took the buck and that was the last hunt we ever had at Tall Tale Deer Camp."

We both sat quietly. I was trying to process

everything. It seemed odd to me that something so wonderful could be ruined over a buck, over one person's greed.

"Did you ever try to talk to J.D., you know, after everything calmed down? I asked.

"No, haven't spoken to him in over thirty years. Some of the other guys used to call and send letters, pleading to open up Tall Tale Deer Camp. But I just couldn't do it, wouldn't be right unless all seven of us were here," said Uncle Ed.

"Does J.D. live around here," I asked.

"J.D.? Oh no, he is way too high class to live in the woods. This isn't no place for a rich boy from Detroit, too many bugs and no room service. Sometimes I think the only reason he came to camp was to try to win by getting the big one. Johnny David Newton can't handle losing, ever!

"Are you talking about *the* Johnny Newton? Like the All-Pro Green Bay Packer quarterback? Is that J.D.?" I asked.

Uncle Ed nodded.

I had no idea, I couldn't believe that the villain who destroyed the deer camp, the once best friend of Uncle Ed, was none other than hall of fame quarterback Johnny Newton.

Everyone in the world knew about Johnny Newton, especially kids from Detroit. He had been a high school football star in Detroit and went on to be a national championship quarterback at the University of Michigan. He was drafted in the first round of the NFL draft by the Green Bay Packers and went on to win three Super Bowls.

He was a legend, a superstar! And he was the one that caused the collapse of Tall Tale Deer Camp...

"There's something we gotta do," I said.

"What's that?" asked Uncle Ed.

"Bring them all back, the original seven members. We need to bring them back for one more deer camp," I said.

~ 27 ~

To my surprise, Uncle Ed was in agreement. There was a hole in his heart, in his soul, ever since the camp closed.

"I still talk to Otis, Big Bob, Tom, and Mickey from time to time. That leaves just Preacher and J.D. of course," he said.

"I will take care of J.D.; you get Preacher here," I said.

We didn't have a lot of time. It was November 8, so we only had seven days to get them here for the opening day of deer season, November 15.

"J.D. won't come, not after what happened," said Uncle Ed.

"Let me worry about Johnny David Newton; you make sure the rest of the guys will be here," I said.

Johnny Newton retired from the National

Football League over 20 years ago. Immediately after retiring he found himself a gravy job as a play-by-play announcer for the Green Bay Packers.

He got paid a ridiculous amount of money to attend and announce all the home games for television. Besides a couple corporate golf outings and autograph signings, Johnny didn't have any obligations.

The Green Bay Packers are more than just a football team to the state of Wisconsin. Because attendance is sold out, getting tickets is almost impossible. Families wait decades just for a chance to own season tickets to the Packers games. The frozen tundra at Lambeau Field is one of the most sacred places in all of football.

We got back to the house and grabbed the newspaper. I looked up the Packers schedule. Luckily, they had a home game this Sunday against my team, the Detroit Lions. I was a die-hard Lions fan. The crazy thing is that almost all of the people in the Upper Peninsula of Michigan are Packer fans because they are closer to Green Bay than they are to Detroit. Lambeau Field was only about a two-hour drive, and it took over seven hours to reach Ford Field where the Lions play.

Yooper's love their Packers, almost as much as they love their pasties and deer hunting. How would I get into the game? I knew it was almost impossible to get tickets.

I asked Uncle Ed and Aunt Loretta, they knew a lot of people with tickets but none that would give one up for me to get into Lambeau Field.

I sat down at the kitchen table. I had to find a way to get there because I had to talk to Johnny Newton.

The phone rang.

"Honey, it's your father," said Aunt Loretta.

Both Mom and Dad called every couple of days to check in on me. The conversations with Mom were mostly short. I still hadn't talked to my dad over the past six weeks. Every time he would call, I would just tell Aunt Loretta I wasn't ready. But this time it was different, I ran to the phone.

"Dad I need your help with something," I said.

I could tell my dad was shocked to hear my voice. I'm sure he thought I wasn't going to talk to him so he was surprised when he heard me on the other end of the phone.

"Sure, Tucker, I'd love to help you with anything," he said.

"I really, really need a ticket to the Packer game this weekend," I said.

"Packer game? I didn't know you liked football," Dad said.

There was no time to explain now. I was eventually going to tell him about the camp and Uncle Ed. I wanted to tell him about the adventure, about shooting my first buck, but I wasn't ready for those types of conversations with him yet.

"Dad, please," I said.

"I might know someone; give me a minute and I'll call you back," he said.

I knew Dad didn't want to disappoint me and was actually excited to be able to do something for me. It had been a long time since he heard any excitement in my voice.

I sat back down at the table and started eating

dinner. About ten minutes later the phone rang; it was my dad.

"Hey, son, I think I might have found you a ticket and a ride. A good friend of mine from Detroit is actually going to the game and has a ticket. He said he'd pick you up on the way. His name is Cameron; he's a great guy," said Dad.

Awesome, for once my dad came through!

Dad added, "He'll pick you up at Uncle Ed's at 8:00 sharp on Sunday, so be ready. One more thing, there's something important I need to talk to you about..."

I thanked him and hung up without even realizing he was still talking.

All I had to do was go to Green Bay, meet a football legend, and convince him to come to the Tall Tale Deer Camp four days after the game. Should be easy, right?

Uncle Ed and I spent the rest of the week cleaning up and getting Tall Tale Deer Camp ready for hunters again. There was a spark to Uncle Ed's steps, and he had a glow about him. I couldn't wait to get home from school so I could go out to camp and help him. It was looking good; it was ready to be alive again.

Saturday morning came early but I didn't even need my alarm clock. I was at the kitchen table eating breakfast before sunrise. Uncle Ed still had a lot of work left at Tall Tale.

"So far I got everyone coming back, only one I haven't been able to talk to is Preacher. Seems no one knows where he is. The last I knew he was a pastor at a small country church in the Thumb, near Kingston," said Uncle Ed.

"We have to get him—everyone has to be here," I said.

"I know, I got a couple phone calls out to his relatives that used to live near Escanaba. I'm sure they'll get back to me soon. You let me worry about Preacher—you worry about J.D.," said Uncle Ed.

I could tell he didn't think there was any way on earth J.D. would ever come back to camp. But deep down, there was a part of Uncle Ed who wanted to see his old friend.

We worked hard all day Saturday getting back

late that night, well after dark. The camp was nearly ready, just a couple small things left.

Exhausted I feel asleep on the couch. I woke up to the smell of Aunt Loretta's pancakes.

It was Sunday morning, and they were getting ready for church. I rolled over and stuffed my face back into my pillow.

I jumped up and looked at the clock, it was 7:30. I rushed to the shower; I had to be ready to go. My ride was coming and I didn't want to make this Cameron guy wait.

Soon I heard tires rolling on the long driveway. I looked out and saw a black Cadillac Escalade with 22 inch chrome rims. The truck was something I would see in Detroit, but never in Plainsville.

Thanks, Dad, I thought to myself. *I get to ride to the Packer game in style.*

I opened the shades and saw the driver's side door open. I almost had a heart attack. I couldn't believe my eyes as my former principal from Washington Carver Middle School stepped out and Mr. David starting strolling towards the front door.

~ 28 ~

Of all the people, this was my dad's friend with the extra ticket! I hadn't seen or talked to Mr. David since he kicked me out of Washington Carver, the day I ruined homecoming with the fake throw-up. I walked over to the door and reluctantly opened it.

"Hello, Tucker," Mr. David said in his deep booming voice. I had heard the voice before.

He could tell I felt awkward; time seemed to stand still as I stood in the doorway searching for a way to apologize.

"You ready to roll, son? The Green Bay Packers don't wait on anybody," he said. He was decked out from head to toe in Packer gear.

I turned and said goodbye to Uncle Ed and Aunt Loretta. He opened the back door to his Escalade and I climbed in.

The truck was full of people. His entire family was there—his wife, Lola, and two boys, Artie and Desmond. I figured they were in fifth or sixth grade. I was shy at first, but after a couple minutes I realized how cool Mr. David and his family were. The boys played games and asked me a bunch of questions. They were funny and interested to learn all about me. Lola was easy to talk to and was genuine. I really liked her.

Mr. David was actually real cool. His music was cool. The way he talked was cool. He had something about him, something I failed to see when I was a student at Washington Carver.

Come to find out, he played three years for the Packers when he was younger. He had been a professional football player but hurt his knee, forcing him to retire early. From there he became a middle school football coach and principal at Washington Carver. Mr. David had grown up in Detroit and actually attended Washington Carver when he was a boy. He told me about his past, how he used to get in trouble before he found God and football. Now I knew why he was so passionate about Washington Carver—it was more than just a school to him.

"Your dad is a good dude, Tucker. We became friends after you came up here. I needed some help with baseball, one of my boys loves baseball. Your dad knows a lot about the game," he said.

Baseball, now there was a game. I loved baseball and had missed it dearly. I thought I would get back at my dad by not playing, but I ended up hurting myself more.

I looked forward to playing baseball again and to talking to my dad. My time away made me realize a lot of things about myself and the divorce. I was tired of being angry and bitter. I loved my parents, even if they were going to be separated. I would have to learn to adjust to it. Being up north gave me time to clear my head and prioritize what really mattered.

Coming up here was the best thing that could have ever happened to me. I was going down the wrong road in Detroit, getting caught up in all the hustle and bustle of city life.

I had changed a lot over the past six weeks, and Uncle Ed and Aunt Loretta were a big reason why. I really enjoyed being with them because I knew they wanted me there.

Now I had to help them—I had to heal Uncle Ed's heartache. I had to repay him for all he had done for me. I had to bring back Tall Tale Deer Camp, not just for Uncle Ed, but for all seven original members. I wanted to experience a deer camp at Tall Tale too.

My jaw dropped as we pulled onto Lombardi Avenue and I saw Lambeau Field for the first time. I had never seen anything so big. Now I could understand why there's so much hype and excitement around the historic field.

In every direction I looked, there was green and yellow. I had never seen so many people, with most of them dressed head to toe in Packer gear complete with gigantic cheesehead hats.

Mr. David pulled into a special, V.I.P. only parking lot. We got out and started walking towards the stadium. Fans kept stopping us along the way—they all wanted pictures with Cameron

"The Tank" David. He was a big celebrity.

As we walked into the stadium, the sound was deafening. The grass almost glowed it was so green, and the stands were packed. The game was about to start, and I was in awe of the whole experience. Lambeau didn't let anyone down.

It was nothing short of amazing. Our seats were almost on the field, four rows up in the end zone. We were surrounded by Packer families and past players.

The players were on the field for the coin toss, and there were television cameras everywhere. There was a desk set up on the sideline below us with two guys sitting there talking into a television camera.

I nudged Mr. David. "Who are they?" I asked, pointing at the broadcasters.

"That's Mike Neely and Johnny Newton," he said.

There was J.D. about ten feet away from me. He was older, about Uncle Ed's age, but looked much different. He didn't look as rough as Uncle Ed. He had a tan, which was odd for Wisconsin in November, and the most perfect white teeth I had ever seen. When he smiled at the camera, they sparkled. It looked like he had just gotten back from a vacation to Hawaii or some tropical island.

"Mr. David, I need one more favor. I need to meet Johnny Newton," I said.

"No problem, Tuck, I can make that happen," he said with a smile.

~ 29 ~

The game was exciting, but Green Bay dominated most of the first half, 28-10.

A Packer player scored a touchdown in our end zone and jumped into the crowd of fans. The famed "Lambeau Leap" is a tradition whenever a Packer scores a touchdown. He jumps into the crowd and gets mobbed by fans. It happened in our section just a couple rows in front of us so we were all on the big screen.

"What does everyone want to eat?" asked Mr. David. Halftime was the best time to get food because no one wanted to leave their seats during the game.

"Tucker, why don't you come with me," he said.

I jumped up and followed him up the steep stairs to the main level where all the food vendors were. We navigated through a bunch of people to a door marked PRIVATE.

He knocked and a large security guard opened the door. He gave Mr. David a huge smile and motioned for us to come in.

We walked into a room filled with food and flat screen televisions. A bunch of people yelled Tank, and Mr. David smiled and gave them high-fives.

He motioned for me to follow him as he worked his way around the room. There was another small door at the back of the room. He opened it and I followed him in.

Two men turned to greet Mr. David, and one was none other than Johnny Newton. At first I was awestruck as he stuck out his hand and smiled like only Johnny Newton could.

I shook his hand and reached into my pocket.

"I'll sign that for you, kid," he said.

Without looking, he grabbed it up. He signed it and went to hand it back as he glanced down at it. To his surprise, it wasn't an old football card like he thought.

It was a picture, a picture of him and Uncle Ed standing in front of the buck pole at Tall Tale Deer Camp. It was a photo from one of the first years of camp, Uncle Ed and J.D. standing with a 4-point buck.

"Where did you get this?" he quickly asked.

"I got it from my Uncle Ed," I said.

His eyes narrowed as he looked down at me.

"Your uncle is Ed McGuffey?" he asked.

I nodded.

"Does he know you have it? Does he know you're here?" he asked.

"Yes, he sent me. He wanted me to invite you back to Tall Tale Deer Camp one more time," I said.

At first he was shocked, you could tell. He wasn't suspecting a visit from Ed's nephew or any talk of Tall Tale Deer Camp. Suddenly his mind was no longer on football. This young kid walked into the room and changed his life. His look of surprise quickly turned to anger.

"Tell him no thanks, kid. I'm not welcome there anymore. You better get going," he said.

I turned to walk away but stopped in the doorway.

"J.D., everyone is going to be there, the original seven," I said.

"J.D. I haven't heard that name in a long time. If you think everyone is going to be there, you're just as crazy as your uncle, that's impossible," he said.

Just before the door shut, I turned and saw Bullwinkle.

There in the corner of his office was the mounted deer head. It was an absolute giant, the biggest deer I'd ever seen. It was mounted proudly as the centerpiece of his office, I knew that was the buck that ended Tall Tale Deer Camp.

Just before the door closed, I yelled "nice trophy." Johnny reached down on his desk and held up his replica Super Bowl trophy.

"Not that one, I meant the one hanging on your wall," I said, motioning to Bullwinkle.

~ 30 ~

"What was that all about?" asked Mr. David.

"Nothing, he's an old friend of my uncle's," I said.

"Old friend, he didn't seem like an old friend. He didn't seem too happy," said Mr. David.

I had failed. I couldn't live up to my end of the deal. I couldn't bring J.D. back to Tall Tale. I went and watched the rest of game. I was thankful I had a chance to come to Lambeau Field but disappointed I couldn't talk J.D. into returning.

I was quiet on the way home. The David family was wonderful, and I felt bad for how I had treated Mr. David and for ruining homecoming.

It was dark when we pulled in. I opened the door and turned to Mr. David.

"Thanks for everything; you have an awesome family," I said.

"No problem, Tuck, we enjoyed taking you."

"I'm sorry about the whole homecoming thing. I'm sorry about a lot of things," I said.

"I know, Tuck, I know. I appreciate it. A simple sorry is powerful. Until I see you again." Mr. David reached out his arm and gave me a fist bump.

I felt better. I had tried to lure J.D. back, experienced a Packer's game, and apologized to someone who deserved it.

The truck backed out and Mr. David rolled down his window.

"Hey, Tuck, forgiving someone is a two-way street. I think it's time you forgave yourself," he shouted as he pulled out onto the main road.

It was time to forgive myself. Deep down, during the entire divorce I did blame myself. I wondered if it was something I had done, or if there was something I could do to stop it.

I went in the house and called my mom. We talked and I opened up about a lot of things. I hung up and called my dad. It was harder to tell my dad, I had so much resentment, so much anger towards him for giving up on our family, for giving up on me.

He cried when I told him that I forgave him. He was carrying that burden for a long time.

I hung up the phone and walked into the living room. Uncle Ed was sitting in his chair reading the local Escanaba newspaper, *The Daily Press*.

"Didn't go too good, huh?" he asked.

I shook my head.

"At least you tried, sometimes I get mad at myself that I never tried early enough. I wonder if it would have all been different if I would have tried to resolve it a long time ago," he said.

There was still someone else that Uncle Ed needed to forgive—himself. It was time to move on and try to salvage any hope of a return by hosting one more deer camp.

"It just won't be the same without J.D., without Preacher," he said.

No Preacher? I thought for sure he would have been able to convince him to come back. Everything I had read about Preacher told me he would be the first in line for a reunion.

"Why didn't Preacher want to come back?"

"Never got a chance to ask him," he said, holding up the newspaper. There in big letters under the heading Obituary read "Douglas "Preacher" Cannon. Preacher had passed away two days ago in a house outside of Grand Rapids.

"I guess I waited too long. I was a couple days too late," said Uncle Ed.

Now it looked like out of the original seven founders of Tall Tale Deer Camp, there would be five coming back. Something seemed to be missing, something wasn't right. The Tall Tale reunion just wouldn't be the same without everyone there.

"Tomorrow I'm going to head out and make the trip to Grand Rapids to pay respect to Preacher. Maybe I can find some forgiveness from him while I'm there," said Uncle Ed.

He added," I know you didn't know him but I want you to go too. You need to meet Preacher."

Although I had never met him in the flesh, I felt like I knew him. The Tall Tale Camp journal had brought all the characters to life from the deer camp.

The next morning we left at 3:00 for Grand Rapids. It was a long drive and I slept most of the way. The funeral was held at the church where Preacher's son is a pastor. His wife, children, and grandchildren were there, and everyone spoke so kindly of him. As the funeral was getting dismissed, the expensive, bright white smile of Johnny Newton caught my eye.

He walked up and hugged Preacher's wife. After a couple minutes of small talk, she reached in her pocket and handed him an envelope. Uncle Ed and J.D. made eye contact but only for a second as J.D. shot him a nasty glare when he left the church.

It was our turn to give our condolences to the family.

"You know, Ed, Preacher loved spending those November weeks with you at deer camp. I would always joke with him, that he loved those 11 days more than the other 354 days of the year," she said with a smile.

A small tear started to well up as they talked and laughed. Just as we turned to leave, she grabbed his arm and pulled out an envelope from her pocket.

"He knew you would be here so he wrote this for you just before he passed," she said. Uncle Ed smiled and took the envelope. We walked out and loaded back into Uncle Ed's truck for the long trek back to the U.P.

A couple minutes into the drive Uncle Ed pulled out the envelope. I recognized the writing from the journal, it was Preacher's. It said, "Ed read at Tall Tale Deer Camp only!"

"I guess we're going to have some entertainment on the 14th," said Uncle Ed.

It only seemed fitting to read it the night before gun season when the other five members met up for the reunion at Tall Deer Camp.

~ 31 ~

November 14th finally arrived. It was a perfect day. There was about an inch of snow on the ground and another cold front moving in—great weather for deer camp.

Aunt Loretta had made a big batch of her homemade pasties, and combined with the campfire, they gave deer camp a magical smell. That morning Uncle Ed and I headed out to camp. Later in the afternoon, the rest of the crew started to arrive. The first was Otis, who was always early. He just couldn't wait; he had missed camp for so long.

Then Mickey and Tom arrived together. It was weird meeting the men I had read about, the ones I had dreamt about sharing deer camp with. All the stories came to life as the men were reunited. It was like time had stood still, and they were just at camp the previous year. The last to pull in was Big Bob. He was a character and quite the story teller. He was a jolly old guy who wore an old-school red and black wool shirt.

The guys set out their guns and put away all the food they had brought. The bunkhouse was full of life and the beds were ready for the first time in thirty years.

Preacher's death was hard on everyone, especially Uncle Ed. He felt a lot of guilt about the way the original camp had ended so many years ago. He was sorry for his part and how he reacted. At this point, it didn't matter who had shot that buck. They all had lost out on thirty years of Tall Tale Deer Camp.

"It's time for Church," Uncle Ed yelled out. They knew to meet at the church, the small out-building that they had all attended on Sundays during deer camp, the same building where Preacher held Sunday services and asked for safety and blessings during deer camp.

The group got up and headed out of the Recreation Room towards Church. The campfire ambers were glowing filling the night sky. I watched as one amber flipped and floated help-lessly towards the stars. The light from the fire illuminated the buck pole and I could picture the deer of the past hanging proudly on it.

There was no doubt, deer camp was a spiritual place, an enchanted place.

We sat down in the pews as Uncle Ed went up to the podium.

"You all know by now of Preacher's passing. He wanted me to read this to everyone tonight, so that's what I am going to do," he said. He was trying not to let his emotions get in the way, but it wasn't working.

He slowly opened the envelope and pulled out a sheet of paper.

November 14th

Finally all the boys are back together. By the grace of God I am in a better place. When Ed called me last week, I couldn't help but smile. I knew I didn't have much time left. For so many years I had waited for the call, the call to have one last trip to Tall Tale Deer Camp. I knew I wouldn't be able to make the trip again, but I wanted to give you one more sermon. I wanted my spirit to sit around the campfire one more time. My days at Tall Tale Deer Camp were some of the best memories I ever had, thank you for that...

Uncle Ed stopped; he couldn't read anymore. The emotions of the reunion and Preacher's death were too much.

"Tucker would you come and finish this?" he said. I was surprised he chose me even though it was uncomfortable, I had to help my Uncle Ed finish what he started. I had to find out what Preacher wanted everyone to know.

As I looked for the words to say, so many came to mind that I had to stop. I wanted to keep things simple; I wanted it to have an impact. I love you guys, I miss you guys, and I know I will see you all again. Enjoy Loretta's pasties, be happy for each other, and pursue a big buck. It's often the little things in life that bring the greatest joy, like spending eleven days in the U.P at deer camp. This was a place for me to clear my mind and purify my soul.

Thanks for the memories, long live Tall Tale Deer Camp! For me, my strength has always been in the scriptures so I am going to leave you with this.

Then Peter came to Jesus and asked, "Lord, how many times shall I forgive my brother when he sins against me? Up to seven times? "Jesus answered, "I tell you, not seven times, but seventy-seven times. Matthew 18: 21-22 NIV

Forever a member,
Preacher

There wasn't a dry eye in Church. The power of forgiveness was something I was experiencing in my own life. It was part of healing, part of living and moving on. It was something that I had to learn. I had been sent from Detroit to the woods of the Upper Peninsula to find forgiveness or to have it find me.

Just as everyone was wiping their eyes, a loud creaking noise came from the back door. We all turned to see J.D. standing in the doorway outlined by the flames of the campfire behind him. He was holding something in his left arm, but I couldn't see what it was.

Without saying a word, he walked over and mounted Bullwinkle above the fireplace. He returned the buck to where it belonged, where it should have been thirty years ago.

No one ever asked what was in J.D.'s letter, but there was something that pulled on his heart, one last message from Preacher that he needed to hear.

J.D. walked up and hugged Uncle Ed, and it was like a huge weight was lifted off both men. Everyone could see years of guilt and shame leave both men.

With that simple act, our mission was complete. We had succeeded in bringing all seven

original members back to Tall Tale Deer Camp
for one last time.

November 25th

*The last eleven days have been some of the
greatest days of my life. The food has been amazing, I think I gained ten pounds. I have never
laughed so much.*

*We got four bucks and three does, with J.D.
shooting a big 10 point. We had an official cere-
mony last night making me a member, now Tall
Tale Deer Camp has seven active members once
again.*

*Tomorrow I am heading back to Detroit. I had
a surprise waiting for me at Uncle Ed's. My parents made the trip up to Plainsville, but this time
they rode up together. Not everything is perfect,
but they are going to work it out, and I couldn't
be happier. They both realized they weren't
ready to quit on their marriage or on our family.
Just like I learned at Tall Tale, it's never too late
to forgive. It's time to go back to Washington
Carver. I think this time it might go a little differ-*

ently. I look forward to seeing Mr. David again and plan on playing baseball this spring.

I wouldn't trade my time up north for anything in the world, except maybe a car ride home with my parents. Until next year...

—Tucker

About the Author

Lane Walker is an award-winning author, speaker, and educator. His book collection, Hometown Hunters, won a Bronze Medal at the Moonbeam Awards for Best Kids series.

Lane is an accomplished outdoor writer in Michigan. He has been writing for the past 15 years and has over 250 articles professionally published. Walker has a real passion for hunter recruitment and getting kids in the outdoors. He is a former teacher and current principal living in Michigan with his wife and four kids.

Lane is a highly sought after professional speaker traveling to schools, churches and wild game dinners.

To book Lane for an event or to find out more check out www.lanewalkerbooks.com or contact him at info@lanewalkerbooks.com.